Reader, Teller and Teacher
The Narrator of Robert Henryson's Moral Fables

SCOTTISH STUDIES

PUBLICATIONS OF THE SCOTTISH STUDIES CENTRE OF THE JOHANNES GUTENBERG UNIVERSITÄT MAINZ IN GERMERSHEIM

General Editor: Horst W. Drescher

Bd./Vol.15

Peter Lang

Frankfurt am Main · Berlin · Bern · New York · Paris · Wien

Rosemary Greentree

Reader, Teller and Teacher
The Narrator of Robert Henryson's
Moral Fables

Peter Lang
Frankfurt am Main · Berlin · Bern · New York · Paris · Wien

Die Deutsche Bibliothek - CIP-Einheitsaufnahme

Greentree, Rosemary:

Reader, teller and teacher : the narrator of Robert Henryson's
Moral fables / Rosemary Greentree. - Frankfurt am Main ;
Berlin ; Bern ; New York ; Paris ; Wien : Lang, 1993
  (Scottish studies ; Vol. 15)
  ISBN 3-631-46552-1

NE: GT

ISSN 0723-2640
ISBN 3-631-46552-1

© Verlag Peter Lang GmbH, Frankfurt am Main 1993
All rights reserved.

Typeset in LATEX at the University of Adelaide

Printed in Germany 1 2 3   5 6 7

FOR RUSSELL,
JAMES AND ANDREW

Contents

ACKNOWLEDGEMENTS

I am happy to acknowledge the help I have received. This work is based on my MA thesis, and has benefited from assistance given in the Barr Smith Library, particularly by Ms Liz Lee, and from the stimulating guidance of my supervisors, Dr Tom Burton and Mr Philip Waldron. I am especially grateful for Dr Burton's generous help in the stages of preparation for publication and Mrs Judith Smith's perceptive reading of the manuscript. Through all the stages I have been encouraged by the love and support of my husband and sons, to whom this work is affectionately dedicated.

ABBREVIATIONS

ASLS	Association for Scottish Literary Studies
AUR	*Aberdeen University Review*
CE	*College English*
ChauR	*Chaucer Review*
CritI	*Critical Inquiry*
DalR	*Dalhousie Review*
diss.	dissertation
DOST	*Dictionary of the Older Scottish Tongue*
EETS	Early English Text Society
EIC	*Essays in Criticism*
ES	*English Studies*
Innes Rev	*Innes Review*
JPC	*Journal of Popular Culture*
LSE	*Leeds Studies in English*
MÆ	*Medium Ævum*
MLN	*Modern Language Notes*
MS	*Mediaeval Studies*
MSpr	*Moderna Språk*
N&Q	*Notes and Queries*
Neophil	*Neophilologus*
NMS	*Nottingham Medieval Studies*
n.s.	new series
OED	*Oxford English Dictionary*
PCP	*Pacific Coast Philology*
RenQ	*Renaissance Quarterly*
RES	*Review of English Studies*
SAQ	*South Atlantic Quarterly*
SLJ	*Scottish Literary Journal*
SP	*Studies in Philology*
SSL	*Studies in Scottish Literature*
STS	Scottish Text Society
TLS	*Times Literary Supplement*
TSLL	*Texas Studies in Language and Literature*
UP	University Press

ABBREVIATIONS

ASLS   Association for Scottish Literary Studies
AUR   Aberdeen University Review
CE   College English
ChauR   Chaucer Review
CritI   Critical Inquiry
D&R   Dahood: Reeve
diss   dissertation
DOST   Dictionary of the Older Scottish Tongue
EETS   Early English Text Society
EIC   Essays in Criticism
...   ...
...   ...
...   ...
MLA   Modern Language ...
MS   Medieval Studies
...Spk   Moral and Spoke
N&Q   Notes and Queries
Viator   Viator ...
PMLA   Publications of the Modern ...
    new series
...   ...
PPhil   Renaissance Philology
RenQ   Renaissance Quarterly
RES   Review of English Studies
SAQ   South Atlantic Quarterly
SLJ   Scottish Literary Journal
SP   Studies in Philology
SSL   Studies in Scottish Literature
STS   Scottish Text Society
TLS   Times Literary Supplement
TSLL   Texas Studies in Language and Literature
UP   University Press

I
Introduction

A narrator is essential to the telling of a story, and may be as conspicuous or as imperceptible as the author desires. In seeking to influence
members of an audience, a narrator may address them directly or try to
affect them merely by the style of narration. The narrator of Henryson's
Moral Fables, whom I shall call the Narrator, uses techniques of persuasion, both direct and indirect, as he tells the tales he attributes to Aesop
and then teaches the lessons he finds in them. He acts as reader, teller and
teacher; and my work will concern his performance in these three capacities.

As reader and teller, the Narrator serves as the window through which
the audience may gain an experience of the fanciful world of the tales. He
links this world with that of his audience, bringing the fantastic tales of the
reasoning, speaking beasts to the reasoning, speaking people who attend
to him, and he moves between their worlds. He must find the truth hidden
in the patent fiction of the fables, and deliver it in the *moralitates* which
follow the tales. As a teacher, he demonstrates and juggles with the truth,
and arranges the moral lessons which he gives to erring man.

The Narrator of the *Moral Fables* is the device Henryson uses to transmit the tales and their lessons to his chosen audience, and it is tempting
to look for some traces of the author in his creation.[1] We may, therefore,
briefly consider what we know of Henryson and his times to see whether
such traces are to be found. Any specific biographical criticism of the *Moral
Fables* would necessarily be very speculative, and I shall not attempt it. We
can be sure of very little that is written of Henryson's life; but we can probably safely accept that he was master of the Abbey School at Dunfermline
and flourished in the latter part of the fifteenth century, during the reigns
of James III and James IV, a time of political turbulence and some social
changes, followed by a more peaceful period. Dunbar's "Lament for the
Makars" suggests that his death, or at least a serious illness, had occurred
before the death of Stobo, in 1505.[2] The record of admission of a Robert

---

[1] We may agree with the view of Wayne C. Booth: "The author's judgement is always
present, always evident to anyone who knows how to look for it ... Though the author
can to some extent choose his disguises, he can never choose to disappear" (Booth, 1961:
20).

[2] "In Dumfermelyne he Death] has done roune / With Maister Robert Henrisoun"
(81–82); "And he has now tane last of aw / Gud gentill Stobo and Quintyne Schaw"
(85–86) (Kinsley, 1979: 180).

Henryson to the senate of the University of Glasgow in 1462 and the occurrence of this name as a witness to documents, as a notary public of Dunfermline, in 1477 and 1478, are accepted as evidence of the poet by Denton Fox, in his edition of Henryson's works (Fox, 1981: xiii).[3] These findings are regarded more cautiously by W.M. Metcalfe, who accepts only the record of admission, and by G. Gregory Smith, H. Harvey Wood, Charles Elliot and Douglas Gray (Metcalfe, 1917: xvii–xviii; Smith, 1914: xxiii; Wood, 1958: xiii; Elliot, 1974: xxiv; Gray, 1979: 3). The poet's works and these historical details suggest an author of liberal education, accustomed to a certain authority, who had a wish to teach. Such a description seems also to apply to his creation, the Narrator. Sir Francis Kinaston's translation of "The Testament of Cresseid" into Latin verse includes a "merry, though somewhat unsavoury tale" of Henryson's death bed, which has its appeal and is frequently quoted, but we may probably only hope that it is true (Wood, 1958: xiii; Gray, 1979: 3; Fox, 1981: xiv).

We may assume Henryson's great familiarity with Aesop's *Fables*, used for the first exercises in Latin translation by school pupils, and also that his works were likely to be read by individuals, rather than be read to groups, as was the case for earlier poets. In style, they are well suited to oral delivery and the Narrator's presence seems always to be that of a speaking voice: recounting, cajoling or admonishing, sharing thoughts of amusement or despair. We may be tempted to think of the Narrator as a *persona* with a pedagogical outlook; but this is not sufficient reason to assume that he is doing no more than stating the views to be expected of the schoolmaster of Dunfermline. Henryson could write, with apparent ease, in a range of styles, a proposition we can verify by reading such varied works as "The Testament of Cresseid," "Orpheus and Eurydice," "Robene and Makyne" and "Sum Practysis of Medecyne."[4] The *Moral Fables* have applications beyond the lessons of the schoolroom, and are to be appreciated by adults, already acquainted with Aesop and his maxims, and prepared to accept that such tales will be accompanied by *moralitates*. The presence of these appendages has disturbed some twentieth-century readers of the work.

In considering the telling of the *Fables* we must also consider the order of the telling, including the question of whether a particular order is to be preferred. If we think of the *Moral Fables* simply as a collection of stories which may not be complete, then any order is possible and none is necessary.[5] The

---

[3] This edition of Henryson's works is cited throughout.

[4] We may discount Metcalfe's prim comment on "Sum Practysis of Medecyne":"it is clear that the author is out of his element" (Metcalfe, 1917: 295).

[5] These views are expressed by John MacQueen and I.W.A. Jamieson, who advocate the use of the Bannatyne Manuscript as a source, rather than the Bassandyne Print (MacQueen, 1967: 189–199; Jamieson, 1974: 31).

witnesses which give all the fables—the Harleian Manuscript and the Bassandyne, Charteris, Hart and Smith Prints—give them in the order shown
in Table 1, which is considered traditional. This order is used in the editions of Metcalfe, Smith, Wood (the first editor to consult the Bassandyne
Print), Elliot, and Fox.

There are three other witnesses: the Bannatyne, Asloan and Makculloch
Manuscripts, and none gives all the fables. The Bannatyne Manuscript has
more of these than the other two, and some of its readings are preferred to
those of any other witnesses. However, it supplies only ten of the fables, and
there are several interpolations in the fifth part of the Manuscript, "con-
tenyng the fabillis of Esop with diuerss upir fabillis and poetical workis
maid & Compyld be diuers lernit men" (Ritchie, 1930: 116). Bannatyne
arranged these works as shown in Table 2, after his own address "To the
redar." Bannatyne's order presents structural and thematic unity for Henryson's *Fables* only in placing together "The Prologue" and "The Cock and
the Jasp," and in the sequence of the three fox fables: "The Cock and the
Fox," "The Fox and the Wolf" and "The Trial of the Fox," where internal
evidence suggests such placement.[6] The fables omitted are those which follow "The Lion and the Mouse" in complete witnesses: "The Fox, the Wolf,
and the Cadger," "The Fox, the Wolf, and the Husbandman" and "The
Wolf and the Wether."

The Bassandyne order is to be preferred on the basis of structural and
thematic evidence and on that of the development of Henryson's sources.
H.H. Roerecke has described the structural unity and symmetry of the
Moral Fables, including the balance of fables of Aesopic and Reynardian
origin, those concerning predators and victims, and those telling of carni-
vores and herbivores (Roerecke, 1969). He sees "The Lion and the Mouse"
as the central point of the fable cycle, and describes a concentric and balanced arrangement of the fables around it. R.J. Lyall writes of Henryson's
development of and divergence from his sources, and proposes an order in
which the *Fables* may have been written, suggesting that Bannatyne may
have used an incomplete version when he compiled his manuscript (Lyall,
1985). In addition to these considerations, thematic development may be
traced in the *Fables*, and I shall present evidence of this type. This development is shown in Henryson's use of recurring imagery, the cumulative
effect of the evolution of character and symbolism, an increasingly sceptical

---

[6] The last lines of "The Prologue," "And to begin, first of ane cok he wrate, / Seikand
his meit, quhilk fand ane iolie stone / Of quhome the fabill ʒe sall heir anone" (61–63),
anticipate "The Cock and the Jasp." The lines "And speik we off the fatall auenture
/ And destenie that to this foxe befell" (616–617) in the first stanza of "The Fox and
the Wolf" refer to "The Cock and the Fox." Similarly, "The Trial of the Fox" begins by
speaking of "[t]his foirsaid foxe that deit for his misdeid" (796), a reference to the fox of
"The Fox and the Wolf."

Table 1   The Bassandyne Order

	The Prologue
I	The Cock and the Jasp
II	The Two Mice
III	The Cock and the Fox
IV	The Fox and the Wolf
V	The Trial of the Fox
VI	The Sheep and the Dog
VII	The Lion and the Mouse
VIII	The Preaching of the Swallow
IX	The Fox, the Wolf, and the Cadger
X	The Fox, the Wolf, and the Husbandman
XI	The Wolf and the Wether
XII	The Wolf and the Lamb
XIII	The Paddock and the Mouse

Table 2   The Bannatyne Order

Henryson	The Preaching of the Swallow
Holland	The Buke of the Howlat
Henryson	The Cock and the Fox
Henryson	The Fox and the Wolf
Henryson	The Trial of the Fox
Henryson	Orpheus and Eurydice
Henryson	The Bludy Serk
Henryson	The Prologue
Henryson	The Cock and the Jasp
Henryson	The Paddock and the Mouse
Henryson	The Two Mice
Henryson	The Sheep and the Dog
Henryson	The Wolf and the Lamb
Henryson	The Lion and the Mouse
Dunbar	The Thrissil and the Rois
Dunbar	The Goldyn Targe
Anon.	The Three Friars of Berwick
	(sometimes doubtfully attributed to Dunbar)
Anon.	Cockelbie Sow
Henryson	Robene and Makyne
Bellenden	The Second Prologue or Proheme of the
	History of the Chronicles of Scotland

[handwritten marginal note:] Begins wholly regative but gets brighter

and ironic treatment of the truth within the fables, and the changing site and function of the Narrator, whose presence gives unity to the work. The later *moralitates* show an elaboration and varied restatement of the lessons of the earlier fables, leading to the complex and detailed statements of the *moralitas* of "The Paddock and the Mouse." The themes are strands repeated and elaborately interwoven as the tales are told and their lessons are taught.

As the fable sequence proceeds, we may see the effects of the Narrator on the tales and of the tales on the Narrator. In "The Prologue" he seems at first to be a storyteller in the conventional, deferential style, presenting to his audience the old, familiar fables of a respected author. As the work progresses, we notice changes in his mood; I shall refer in particular to those of his first and very important contact with the audience, in "The Prologue" and "The Cock and the Jasp," which establish the relationship between the Narrator and his audience. Later fables show his feelings towards the characters of the tales and the humans they represent, and his teaching in the *moralitates* reveals still more of his attitudes towards mankind in general and the individuals he may pity or despise, but cannot ignore, even when he sees little hope for an improvement in this life.

The early fables generally suggest that justice is possible, and reach a peak of optimism at the mid-point of the work, in "The Lion and the Mouse," the fable told by Aesop, in a dream vision. The fables which come after this depict a world without justice, where man's only hope can be for a happier after-life. Small wonder that the Narrator's mood is one of increasing pessimism, and that humour in these later tales is cruel, grim and scanty, derived from such sources as the duping and beating of the wolf and the ironic remarks of the deluded lark. We can gain little enjoyment from the brief triumph of the disguised wether, and we must feel, as we read the fables of the second half of the work, that only the guileful and the vicious can have any success. These fables have many victims; and, although we feel no pity for the wolf when the fox leads him to misfortune, we share the sorrow of the Narrator when he tells the tales of more endearing and helpless creatures, such as the unheeding birds, the lamb and the mouse.

For a number of reasons, then, the style of telling the *Fables* is important in the teaching of their lessons, and the Narrator and the order of telling are aspects of that style. I shall write in greater detail of the effects of recurring themes and imagery, and consider the wolf as a particular example of the development of character and symbolism. The development of the Narrator's themes confirms the traditional or Bassandyne order of the *Fables* and the notion that the collection is a completed work. Greatest attention will be given to the Narrator, because his constant presence gives unity and continuity to the work and his darkening mood is the most significant influence on the tone of the *Fables*, as he moves from the fabulous to the realistic, from the world of the tales to the world of men.

II
The Narrator gains his audience

The opening of Robert Henryson's *Moral Fables* serves the important purpose of introducing the Narrator and his fables to the audience, but it must do more than that. The Narrator must, at the outset, establish a relationship which will allow him to guide the thoughts of his listeners to conclusions which may be unexpected, while he tells tales which have long been familiar. This is a relationship of dependence, and its development may be seen in "The Prologue" and in the fable which follows it, "The Cock and the Jasp." Although variations in the witnesses may prompt questions about the order of the *Fables*, there can be no doubt that the last stanza of "The Prologue" announces and precedes "The Cock and the Jasp":

> And to begin, first of ane cok he wrate,
> Seikand his meit, quhilk fand ane iolie stone,
> Of quhome the fabill ʒe sall heir anone.   (61–63)

The fable is traditionally the first told in Aesopic cycles, as for example, in the collections of Gualterus Anglicus and Lydgate, and it illustrates its protagonist's unsound judgement, implying a need for direction. "The Prologue" and "The Cock and the Jasp" are related not only in proximity and in beginning the dependence of the audience on the Narrator, but also in their ironic tone, which is established in "The Prologue," exploited in "The Cock and the Jasp" and continues thereafter to inform the other fables. These two parts of the fable cycle may be considered together as the opening section of the whole work, preparing the audience for the Narrator's interpretation of all that follows. "The Cock and the Jasp" differs from the other fables in telling of no perceived threat to its protagonist, who is not aware of the significance of his adventure and so learns no lesson. The moral teaching is given only to the audience, and thus the audience must depend on the Narrator.

He offers little in the tales which is new, but manipulates his public's knowledge to apprehend *moralitates* which may surprise them. The first assumption about his audience could certainly be that they already knew the fables. Those attributed to Aesop were used as exercises in Latin translation for school pupils, and they and beast stories taken from the *Roman de Renart* were frequently found as *exampla* in sermons. The scantiness of the descriptive passages in the tales reinforces the notion of the audience's familiarity with them. A fable such as "The Cock and the Fox" can be seen to draw on descriptions previously heard. Henryson's "gentill Chante-cleir" is described only in the brief, flattering and unreliable allusions of Lowrence, the fox; but the audience's idea of him must owe much to memories of Chaucer's gorgeous Chauntecleer, pictured in such detail in "The Nun's Priest's Tale." Henryson's "Prologue," addressed to his Narrator's "maisteris," implies a more relaxed audience than those of the church or schoolroom, but their first acquaintance with fables would prepare them to be taught as well as amused. We are always aware of the Narrator's voice, and may consider ourselves part of his audience, even when reading the *Fables* silently and privately. In a work where the stories are advanced largely through speeches, he is the speaker who has the longest and most influential part.

As the demeanour of the Narrator varies, so must the response he is seeking from the audience. He begins with a justification of fables, giving the standard argument that their pleasant style attracts man's interest, although they are improbable fictions. The first few lines of the stanza flow smoothly, with soft and unobtrusive alliteration of "s" and "p" sounds:

> Thocht fein3eit fabils of ald poetre
> Be not al grunded vpon truth, 3it than,
> Thair polite termes of sweit rhetore
> Richt plesand ar vnto the eir of man; (1–4)

but the movement becomes more difficult as the reason for the fables is given, "als the caus quhy thay first began" (5), and is completely jarred by the concluding lines, "Wes to repreif the of thi misleuing, / O man, be figure of ane vther thing" (6–7). The alliterative combination of "f" and "th" now serves to retard and emphasize the words.[1] There must be a change in pace and mood, to parallel turning from bland lines of reference to an undisputed statement about false fables to giving a stern reproach of those to whom the teaching is directed. Such reversals and surprises play a significant part in Henryson's technique, with abrupt changes in mood and tone used to produce startling effects, both dramatic and comic (Roerecke, 1969: 70–88).

The Narrator continues concisely, always implying more than he says, relying on the audience to supply details, as he speaks of the field and its grain, the nutshell and its kernel, and the benefit of refreshment for the mind, using the metaphor of the bent bow. These are familiar concepts,

---

[1] The reading "the of thi misleuing / O man," which follows a suggestion made by G.G. Smith, is more vigorous and direct than "the haill misleving / Off man," found in the editions of Elliot and Wood. Fox explains his emendation in a note on lines 6–7 (Fox, 1981: 189). It is closest to the version of the Makculloch MS, "þe of þi myslewyng / of man" (Stevenson, 1918: 3).

illustrated by familiar figures. In the hands of another poet, they might have been amplified with detailed descriptions and particular cases. Henryson however, uses them with restraint, so keeping attention focused on the introduction of the fables, rather than extraneous distractions of scenery or characters. This method is used throughout the *Fables*, where descriptions and metaphors are generally brief, with details added only to transfer the tales from the stateless, timeless world of Aesop and the *milieu* of Renart to Henryson's setting of Scotland in the fifteenth century, as seen in the descriptive passages in "The Lion and the Mouse" and "The Preaching of the Swallow."

The first figure, of the field to be tilled, suggests the hard work needed to win its crops and may also imply the efforts of the audience to gain the messages of the fables, the less evident ones as well as those which are frankly stated. The metaphor of the shell and kernel which follows has connotations of religious symbolism beyond its most obvious interpretation of a core of meaning within a useless husk, a valuable truth to be retained when fiction has been discarded.[2] Thus the brief reference,

> The nuttis schell, thocht it be hard and teuch,
> Haldis the kirnell, sueit and delectabill;
> Sa lyis thair ane doctrine wyse aneuch
> And full of frute, vnder ane fenჳeit fabill;   (15–18)

implies a good deal of meaning and also the engagement of receptive and discerning minds. The concise style of the Narrator places the importance of these familiar figures an ironic light. He appears to mention them for the sake of convention, but moves quickly to other matters.

We may compare Henryson's conciseness with the copious style of Lydgate, as it is seen in his *Isopes Fabules*. His "Prologue and Fable I" resembles "The Prologue" and "The Cock and the Jasp" in stanza form and matter, but we find more differences than similarities when we compare the styles of the two poets. Lydgate's is an exhaustive one. He is unrestrained in his introduction of Aesop, who is simply mentioned by Henryson's Narrator as his author, making introduction and justification seem unnecessary. A striking difference is seen in Lydgate's expansion of the complex figures he uses, exemplified in a stanza describing the winning of wisdom from fables:

---

[2] E.N. Daugherty notes that the figure is associated with the story of Aaron's rod which produced almonds (Numbers 17, 8), and that the nutshell and kernel symbolize the crucifixion and salvation (Daugherty, 1977: 1). J. Huizinga describes the elaborate symbolism suggested by the walnut: "The walnut signifies Christ; the sweet kernel is His divine nature, the green and pulpy outer peel is His humanity, the wooden shell between is the cross" (Huizinga, 1979: 198).

> Vnder blak erþ byn precious stones founde,
> Ryche saphyres & charbuncles full ryall,
> And, who þat myneþ downe lowe in þe grounde,
> Of gold & syluer groweþ þe mynerall;
> Perlys whyte, clere & orientall
> Ben oft founde in muscle shellys blake,
> And out of fables gret wysdom men may take.
>
> (McCracken, 1934: 567, lines 22–28)

The elaborate mass of details reduces the importance of each detail to an equivalent and hence a slight significance. The mind's eye is dazzled by the gaudy images of jewels and precious metals, offset by the contrasting blackness of earth and oyster shells. One must also think of the operations of mining and taking pearls. So many considerations must take the audience's attention from the course of Lydgate's teaching. In contrast, Henryson's economical metaphors have little to distract the audience from the line of his argument, although they imply a wealth of previous knowledge. Their overwrought style makes the eight stanzas of Lydgate's "Prologue" seem longer than the nine of Henryson's. The most significant difference in content between the two works is Lydgate's omission of any direct reproof to erring man. The mood expressed here does not appear to change as does that of Henryson's Narrator.

The relationship between the Narrator and his audience varies in "The Prologue," becoming established through a number of approaches. It is far from the intimate one which may be inferred from the concluding stanza of the last fable, "The Paddock and the Mouse," which begins "Adew, my freind" (2969). The Narrator begins "The Prologue" blandly, then speaks sternly, with the admonition, as from the pulpit, "of thi misleuing." He becomes apparently deferential and tentative in the conventional display of modesty with which he introduces himself, beginning "my maisteris, with ȝour leif, / Submitting me to ȝour correctioun" (29–30). The passage tells of his allegedly scanty knowledge of Latin and rhetoric, asks his gracious audience to correct his errors and asserts that he has translated the fables only at the request "of ane lord, / Of quhome the name it neidis not record" (34–35). This obligatory exercise in diffidence is also an example of amplification, which slows the movement of the verse and emphasizes the presence of the Narrator through the repetition of personal pronouns. As he submits himself, excuses his negligence and apologizes for his shortcomings, he uses eight personal pronouns between lines 29 and 40. This exaggerated modesty is not self-effacing, and may amuse or flatter, as does similarly extravagant humility employed by the fox in later fables, but it could not be taken at face value. Greater compliments to the audience's knowledge and perception are suggested elsewhere by the Narrator's brevity.

He continues to speak as a translator, merely the instrument of his author, as he tells Aesop's stories of beasts with the human qualities of speech and reason, but becomes more bold when he suggests that "mony men in operatioun / Ar like to beistis in conditioun" (48–49). The next stanza, describing man as "lyke ane beist, / Quhilk lufis ay carnall and foull delyte" (50–51), implies that, far from deferring to his fellow man, the Narrator despises him, at least in his beastly aspects. He no longer speaks of animals with human qualities which "to gude purpois dispute and argow" (45), but, with contempt, of the reverse transformation, which may continue until man is unrestrained by shame and "in brutal beist is transformate" (56). (The progressively degenerative influence of sin is the theme of a later fable, "Thc Prcaching of the Swallow.") After this uncompromising rebuke, the Narrator concludes "The Prologue" as mildly as he began it, by announcing the first fable, "The Cock and the Jasp."

The changes in demeanour suggest ironic inconsequence, as the Narrator speaks blandly of false fables, jolts his listeners with a stern reproof, runs through a stock of familiar metaphors, conventionally deprecates himself and flatters his audience, then, with the authority of his author, condemns the beastliness of man and announces his first fable. What can we make of such swings of mood in one who condemns, converses, cajoles and then condemns more strongly, all within a few stanzas? His range of attitudes hints that he is not only a translator, teacher, preacher or entertainer. He must be all of these, and states his intention "[w]ith sad materis sum merines to ming" (26). Thus the relationship established with the audience in "The Prologue" is variable, developing into one which demands the audience's dependence on the Narrator's judgement and guidance. We may think that Henryson is ridiculing the whole form of the conventional prologue by displaying such a variety of manners, but this would be an exaggerated view. The changes in his composure undercut both the overwrought humility and the stern reproaches, suggesting an ironic temper of mind which should warn against taking all that follows at face value. However, although opposites are seen, the Narrator's comments do not simply cancel out. Rigorous moralizing appears too often to be ignored, but the ironies in his approaches should prepare us to look warily at the *Fables* and not give our sympathies too readily. Mankind, as represented by the animals of the tales, will be seen ironically, and the audience may be carried along by the Narrator's words and implications only to find them contradicted by later pronouncements, as in "The Cock and the Jasp" which follows and exemplifies the Narrator's style.

The first reasoning beast, the cock, has a disconcerting mixture of qualities, with those representing animal and human aspects of his nature very evenly balanced. It seems that we need some degree of overbalance to see

12

an animal character as representing man in a convincing way. We may, for example, compare the character of this cock with that of Chantecleir, who appears in "The Cock and the Fox." Chantecleir's physical description, as previously mentioned, is minimal, and it is irrelevant to the story. The tale concerns the human qualities which he represents, and these are clearly and delightfully exposed. Although his intellectual processes are vital to the story, the colours of his feathers are insignificant, and may be supplied from memory or imagination if required by the audience. Similarly, Lowrence's appearance is described in detail only when he employs his trick of pretending death, in "The Fox, the Wolf, and the Cadger," and this, like his other actions, is a product of the intellect and personality on which all the fox stories are based.

The balance of the cock's characteristics has an oddly disturbing effect; he reasons in human style but with an animal's level of discernment, and bases his thoughts on animal premises. The brief description of his appearance, "with feddram fresch and gay" (64) is unambiguously animal, as is flying forth to scrape in the dunghill for his food; but "cant and crous" (65) can be used of humans as well as animals, and may suggest a jaunty boldness or objectionable smugness.[3] His motive, "[t]o get his dennar" (67), is similarly ambiguous, a universal need of beasts and men, and the jasp might have been found by any animal or person looking in that place. Since careless housemaids may have swept out the stone, they might also need to look for it. The cock's poverty and his urge to address the jasp sound human, but his rhetorical flights of fancy are always undercut by descents into bathos, intruding into the inflated speeches and reflecting the beastliness which taints man's nature. Consider the dramatic conclusion to his address, with its rising anaphora falling to prosaic depths:

'Quhar suld thow mak thy habitatioun?
Quhar suld thow duell, bot in ane royall tour?
Quhar suld thow sit, bot in ane kingis croun
Exalt in worschip and in grit honour?
Rise, gentill Iasp, of all stanis the flour,
Out of this fen, and pas quhar thow suld be;
Thow ganis not for me, nor I for the.'   (106–112)

The abrupt changes in tone recall those of "The Prologue." The cock begins so grandly, but can never rise far above the level of his midden. His speech juxtaposes such contrasts in "habitatioun" as "royall tour" and "fen," but

---

[3] Fox notes that the phrase "cant and crous" suggest heroic boldness in *Cronicillis of Scotland* 35915, and "crous" is used in Ferguson's Scottish Proverbs, 1641 edn., to describe a cock and a louse. Applications of the adjective to cocks appear in *OED* and *DOST* (Fox, 1981: 196).

he does nothing to remove the jasp from its unworthy situation or to use it for his own benefit. The jingling last line of the stanza, with which he dismisses the jasp, confirms his preference for something which is obviously of immediate use to himself. We might expect a cock of greater discernment to return the jasp or sell it for gain, or perhaps be inspired to seek his food more boldly outside the farmyard. Such ideas borrow from the world of men no more fancifully than that of a fox who casts his horoscope and then confesses his sins as a precaution against disaster, as Lowrence does in "The Fox and the Wolf." We can agree with Clark that "in sober fact, a real cock who carried a precious stone into a jeweller's shop or kept it about his person would be more likely to be stuffed with sage than sagacity" (Clark, 1976: 8), but this is a "feinʒeit fable," not sober fact. The cock's speech reveals that he realizes something of the jasp's worth, and so he is judged for the limits of his knowledge and the actions it inspires in him.

His words make a puzzling tangle of threads of reasoning which apply to beasts and to men. We need to be guided through this tangle if we are to understand the tale and its *moralitas*, and our guide must be the Narrator. The cock finds a jewel which is of no use to a bird in need of food, but he does not simply push it aside in his search for something edible. Instead, he addresses it, as might a man, speaking of its material value and beauty as well as its uselessness to himself. He is aware of its worth in terms of "sa mekill gold" (84) and "confort to the sicht" (100), but does not exploit these characteristics and does not discern its symbolic and spiritual qualities. These are described by the Narrator in the *moralitas*, in eloquence of sustained tone. We may compare his exemplary human response, as it is shown in the passage which tells of the benefits of wisdom, symbolized by the jasp, with that part of the cock's speech quoted above:

> Quha may be hardie, riche, and gratious?
> Quha can eschew perrell and auenture?
> Quha can gouerne ane realme, cietie, or hous
> Without science? No man, I ʒow assure.
> It is riches that euer sall indure,
> Quhilk maith, nor moist, nor vther rust can freit:
> To mannis saull it is eternall meit.   (134–140)

There are resemblances in the constructions used in the two stanzas, and the references to governing the realm may recall the cock's talk of the "kingis croun"; but there are revealing differences in the styles and values of the two speakers. The Narrator's intrusion, "I ʒow assure," reminds us of his presence, but it seems slight and disinterested when compared with the cock's urgent and pervasive self-interest. The mundane realities of "maith," "moist" and "vther rust" are mentioned only as factors which cannot prevail, and the stanza ends with a positive affirmation of the jasp which the cock has rejected. It is seen as the symbol of "eternall meit," a lasting food for the spirit, unlike the scraps for which the cock must search every day. Of course the Narrator is speaking of its value to man whereas the cock is concerned with its value to himself, but this fable exemplifies the variable and ironic standards of the Narrator's judgement.

The reasons the cock gives for rejecting the jasp are those of a cock. He needs food, and the "small wormis, or snaillis" (94) which he would prefer to the beautiful jewel were probably, even if irrationally, considered a revolting part of his diet by a medieval audience.[4] But the cock is not intended to be a completely natural bird. He represents man. His argument is of the disquieting kind which seems reasonable as it is delivered, but can be shown to be flawed in retrospect, and with flaws which mock those who did not see them. The *moralitas* of this fable can provoke irritation or disbelief, and perhaps sympathy for a hungry creature obliged in nature only to feed his own body, yet ridiculed for rejecting something of spiritual value to man. Khinoy sums up such responses when he suggests "We may feel cheated" (Khinoy, 1982: 102).

"The Cock and the Jasp" differs from other fables in Henryson's work because its lesson is learned only in the *moralitas*, and by the audience, not by its protagonist. The cock remains unaware of the opportunity and obligation to gain wisdom, and perhaps considers that he has coped well with the inconvenience of finding something inedible during his daily search for food. He is thus an excellent figure for man who, with his imperfect perception, sees only a part of the lessons of the world around him and remains quite satisfied with his ideas of his obligations. A tale illustrating this lack of discernment is a very appropriate one with which to begin the fable cycle, since the success of fables depends on the audience's apprehension of their veiled messages. The difficulties of being shown the cock first as a likeable and amusing character and later simply as an ignorant fool give another example of incomplete perception, this time at the audience's expense. Jolted members of the audience, if not too infuriated, are more likely to be responsive to the Narrator's direction than if the first tale told had been as apparently straightforward as "The Two Mice" and "The Cock and the Fox" which follow, with unsurprising *moralitates* demanding less involvement and self-criticism of the listeners. Our lack of immediate understanding of the moral and our wish to understand it make ways to engage our attention and increase our dependence on the Narrator's guidance. Without the Narrator, the audience could be as undiscerning as the cock.

---

[4] Suggested by Fox (Fox, 1962: 345 and 1981: 197), but denied by Clark (Clark, 1976: 8).

The changes in the Narrator's mood in "The Prologue" are ironically inconsequent, a warning against taking all that follows at face value. We find that this applies to the tales of the *Fables*, although we can accept the *moralitates*, and this is borne out in the fable of "The Cock and the Jasp." The close relation of this fable in style and variation of tone suggest that it may be considered with "The Prologue" as forming the introductory section of the *Moral Fables* when the Narrator gains his audience. The rapid and extreme changes in tone introduced and exemplified here are important in Henryson's technique for attracting and retaining the attention of his audience, as he tells, using the device of the Narrator, stories which are already familiar. As the fable cycle proceeds, the outlook of the stern moralist becomes prominent in the Narrator's range of moods. He seems to show admiration for some of the characters whose failings he later exposes, such as the city mouse whose respectability is ironically displayed in "The Two Mice," and he pities some of the most helpless victims, unmistakably condemning their oppressors, as in "The Wolf and the Lamb." So many failings and injustices are disclosed that the mood of the Narrator appears to be one of growing pessimism. There is much comedy in the early *Fables*, but, as the sequence continues, this becomes more sparse and grim, until it rests on the incongruities which relieve some of the gruesomeness of "The Paddock and the Mouse," the tale of the little mouse who had to trust a wily toad to carry her across a stream because she had no horse to ride. Since the Narrator persists in telling the *Fables*, even when he seems to think that man must look for a better life in heaven, not on earth, we must imagine some place for hope in his penetrating, undeceived view of life. We may assume that, although he despises some of humanity's beastly deeds, he still retains an affection for people, and wants to teach again the lessons of the old fables to an audience whose thoughts he can guide.

III
The Narrator's style

In spite of any wishes, a narrator cannot long be impartial. Unbiased transmission of information is appropriate only to official records and statistics, and even these can be manipulated. What does a narrator do? He does not merely recite actions and describe settings and character. Through narration, he becomes part of the story he tells, and through him the author and the reader transmit, adjust and absorb the tale as it is told. The narrator's is the voice chosen by the author, a creation as are the characters, but although he tells the tales the narrator does not belong to them as do the characters. The Narrator of Henryson's *Fables* is a device used by the author, the voice he chooses for the delivery of the tales and their *moralitates*.

When we read fables we accept the paradox of the truth to be found in fiction. Of course, we recognize the demand for attention whenever we read and respond to an imaginative work and adjust our reception of the work accordingly, but only occasionally must we juggle and accept truth and fiction in this way.[1] It could seem a more difficult paradox without a narrator to guide our way. When we allow Henryson's Narrator full charge of our imaginations we accept the illusions he creates. The first of these is that of entering the world of his audience, the second is that of the world of his characters. Each depends on the other and on the Narrator for existence. The most potent illusion is that we accept the idea of fiction within the world of the characters and truth in that of the audience, the idea that truthful instruction comes to the audience from the outrageous fiction of the tales. When we read the *Fables* we enter the imaginary world of the Narrator's listeners, and prepare ourselves to hear his truths.

The Narrator acts in the *Fables* as reader, teller and teacher of the tales and their morals. He reads the old fables, his sources, and produces a

[1] Walter J. Ong describes "the game of literacy" which readers play, and illustrates it with the following example:

> An office worker on a bus reading a novel of Thomas Hardy is listening to a voice which is not that of any real person in the real setting around him. He is playing the role demanded of him by this person speaking in a quite special way from this book, which is not the subway and is not quite "Wessex" either, although it speaks of Wessex. Readers over the ages have had to learn this game of literacy .... They have to know how to play the game of being a member of an audience that "really" does not exist. (Ong, 1975: 12)

18

version suited to his audience, telling the tales in a way which suggests the presence of a speaking narrator, rather than the style of a distant writer, using tricks of speech and repeated cues to which the audience may respond. As teacher of their lessons, he expounds the morals and delivers many sections of the tales in a pedagogical style, never neglecting his obligation to instruct as he entertains.

The purpose of fables is to illustrate the lessons they carry, and the form in which the instruction is offered must be the one most appropriate for the audience for whom it is intended, sometimes using elaboration or simplification, but still preserving the timeless, universal qualities of the original. Any retelling, perhaps modified, abbreviated or extended, is that narrator's reading of the fable, coloured by his interpretation of the tale and his idea of the moral lessons to be drawn by his contemporaries, revealed in images and phrases as well as in overt comments. Each reading shows something of its narrator, his time and place, as well as transmitting the fable.

We may look, for comparison, at several versions of the fable of "The Two Mice." Henryson's Narrator, his device for taking Aesop's *Fables* to his own time and place, gives a reading for the instruction of a Scottish audience of the fifteenth century. The characters retain their original natures, but are defined by contemporary details. The town mouse is a "gild brother and made ane fre burges" (172), able to go at will "amang the cheis and meill, in ark and kist" (175). The sumptuous feast she presents is a parody of those in medieval romances, "Except ane thing: thay drank the watter cleir / In steid off wyne" (272–273). In Horace's version, the city dweller offers the remains of a Roman feast "like a waiter with tunic girt up, serving course upon course and ... [plays] ... the part of a houseslave to the very life, taking a preliminary lick at every dish" (Handford, 1979: 219). Wyatt gave the same fable in his "Satire 2," ("My mother's maids, when they did sew and spin"), and his version owes much to Horace and probably also to Henryson.[2] His tale, however, is moved to Wyatt's uncertain times, which seem to inspire the message he sends to Poyntz:

There is no gold that may
Grant that ye seek, no war, no peace, no strife—
No, no: although thy head were hooped with gold,
Sergeant with mace, halbert, sword, nor knife
Cannot repulse the care that follows should!
(Daalder, 1975: 107, lines 75–79)

The fable remains, but individual readings emphasize different aspects.

---

[2] Fox discusses the resemblances between Henryson's and Wyatt's versions of the fable, and suggests that both poets were familiar with a Scoto-Danish song, of which a stanza has been found (Fox, 1971).

The telling of the *Fables* reveals the nature and point of view of the Narrator. No doubt he gives Henryson's opinions, but we should beware of thinking that he gives nothing more than the views of the schoolmaster of Dunfermline. We must remember that the Narrator of the *Fables* is as distinct an entity as is the corresponding figure in "The Testament of Cresseid," and it is hard to imagine that Henryson's own personality was the only source of these disparate creations. Each is the guise most suited for the narration of the work, and the poet created such differing masks as the pedagogical moralist and the weary servant of love, allowing scope for acquaintance, enjoyment, mockery or pity of the narrators as the poems proceed.

The Narrator asserts his presence throughout the telling of the *Fables*. Although he is most conspicuous in the three central fables, we must disagree with Fox's implication that these are the only fables in which the Narrator appears and with Burrow's assertion that "The Preaching of the Swallow" is "the only one of the Fables to introduce a human observer into the story" (Fox, 1981: lxxviii; Burrow, 1975: 25). Sometimes his presence is shown in the repetition of first person pronouns, as in "The Prologue" in the lines of exaggerated humility which undermine the obligatory formal flattery of his listeners,

> In hamelie language and in termes rude
> Me neidis write, for quhy of eloquence
> Nor rethorike, I neuer vnderstude.
> Thairfoir meiklie I pray 3our reuerence,
> Gif 3e find ocht that throw my negligence
> Be deminute, or 3it superfluous,
> Correct it at 3our willis gratious.   (36–42)

As he proceeds, he directs the audience's attention to apply the lessons learned from the characters to their own lives. For this purpose he often addresses comments and advice directly, particularly reminding us of his presence in the *moralitates*, with commands such as "Ga seik the iasp, quha will," (161) and "Be war, gude folk, and feir this suddane schoit" (789), or the more gentle instructions: "Freindis, heir may 3e find, will 3e tak heid, / In this fabill ane gude moralitie" (365–366). A digression in the first tale is the earliest sign that our attention will continually be drawn to human affairs, when the tale of a cock is interrupted by speculation about the source of the jasp:

> As damisellis wantoun and insolent
> That fane wald play and on the streit be sene,
> To swoping of the hous thay tak na tent

Quhat be thairin, swa that the flure be clene;
Iowellis ar tint, as oftymis hes bene sene,
Vpon the flure, and swopit furth anone.
Peraduenture, sa wes the samin stone.   (71–77)

The Narrator's asides, often proverbial in tone, express his judgement in the tales as well as in the *moralitates*. We find examples in "The Cock and the Fox," in the description of Chantecleir, "inflate with wind and fals vane gloir, / That mony puttis vnto confusioun" (474–475), and in the stern general comment, "falset failȝeis ay at the latter end" (568), made when Lowrence is outwitted. The flow of narrative is sometimes halted by expostulations which vent the Narrator's anger. "The Trial of the Fox" furnishes examples such as the exclamation "Fy, couetice, vnkynd and venemous!" (817) made when the younger fox rejoices at the inheritance of his father's hunting territory, and the longer outburst condemning the fox's attempt to hide from the lion, when first Lowrence and then the audience must bear the force of the Narrator's words:

O fylit spreit, and cankerit conscience!
Befoir ane roy renȝeit with richteousnes,
Blakinnit cheikis and schamefull countenance!
Fairweill thy fame; now gone is all thy grace!
The phisnomie, the fauour off thy face.
For thy defence is foull and disfigurate,
Brocht to the licht basit, blunt, and blait.

Be thow atteicheit with thift, or with tressoun,
For thy misdeid wrangous, and wickit fay,
Thy cheir changis, Lowrence, thow man luke doun;
Thy worschip of this warld is went away.
Luke to this tod, how he wes in effray,
And fle the filth of falset, I the reid,
Quhairthrow thair fallowis syn and schamefull deid.
                                        (971–984)

Such remarks suggest the immediacy of application of the tales, and reinforce the illusion that the reader has joined the imaginary group receiving the Narrator's attention.

The Narrator is conspicuously before us in the tales of the early fables. His presence is suggested with more restraint in those which follow "The Preaching of the Swallow," although the tone of the narrative continues to indicate his point of view, and remarks directed to the audience are still to be found. "The Wolf and the Lamb" offers illustrations in the subjective introductions of the two characters. The wolf is "cruell ... richt rauenous and fell" (2616); and when he drinks "[t]o slaik his thrist" (2619), his thoughts are "all on wickitnes" (2624). In contrast, we read that "[t]he selie lamb wes meik and innocent" (2625), "[a]nd in the streme laipit to cule his thrist" (2622). The descriptions of the creatures are concise and biased; and their speeches, which make up the greater part of the tale, echo the vicious snarling of the wolf, emphasized by such sounds as "3aa" and "Ha," while mild phrases suggest the meek and futile bleating of the lamb. They may be compared in the stanzas of ferocious and unproved accusation of the lamb's father, spoken by the wolf, and answered in the reasonable but unavailing words of the lamb:

> 'He wraithit me, and than I culd him warne,
> Within ane 3eir, and I brukit my heid,
> I suld be wrokkin on him or on his barne
> For his exorbetant and frawart pleid:
> Thow sall doutles for his deidis be deid.'
> 'Schir, it is wrang that for the fatheris gilt
> The saikles sone suld punist be or spilt.
>
> 'Haiff 3e not hard quhat Halie Scripture sayis,
> Endytit with the mouth off God almycht?
> Off his awin deidis ilk man sall beir the pais,
> As pyne for sin, reward for werkis rycht;
> For my trespas, quhy suld my sone haue plycht?
> Quha did the mis, lat him sustene the pane.'
> '3aa!' quod the volff. '3it pleyis thow agane?'   (2658–2671)

The lamb's speeches give a sad confirmation of Aesop's assertion that "haly preiching may na thing auaill" (1390). The Narrator's feelings are openly expressed in the last lines of the tale:

> Off his murther quhat sall we say, allace?
> Wes not this reuth, wes not this grit pietie,
> To gar this selie lamb but gilt thus de?   (2704–2706)

By using the plural pronoun "we" rather than "I," the Narrator allies himself with his audience, and strengthens his comment with assumed agreement.

Although most teaching is done in the *moralitates*, some lessons are given in the tales, as in the asides and expostulations already mentioned and through the subjective telling of the tales. We are rarely in doubt about obvious villains, such as the fox and wolf, or about victims, such as the sheep characters; but some messages are only clarified in the interpretations which follow the tales. We may think particularly of the surprises and depth of meaning to be found in "The Cock and the Jasp," "The Wolf and the Wether" and "The Fox, the Wolf, and the Husbandman." His style of narration implies the Narrator's teachings throughout the tales. The idiosyncratic, subjective manner gives the effect of a speaking voice, haranguing and pleading, mocking and pitying in turn. He may be amused, angry or sad, praying, condemning or satirizing, but he never seems to present only an impartial or detached record. He may even obscure a significant event among others described in more detail, as in "The Trial of the Fox," where the incident of the mare's kick, described quite briefly in the long tale, is the source of the *moralitas*.

One can imagine the *Fables* being told with great scope for melodramatic delivery and many opportunities for tricks of speech. Most of the tales are told through the words of the characters, with few sustained passages without speech. In spite of the theatrical nature of the speeches, we cannot say with certainty that the *Moral Fables* is a work intended for performance rather than private, silent reading, but we can say that the devices of the stage give the effect of the continually speaking presence we call the Narrator. This enhances the illusion that the reader has joined his audience, prepared to accept the illusory balance of truth and fiction presented by the author. A part of the technique used to create and preserve this effect is the Narrator's use of cues to provoke the audience to recall and anticipate recurring situations in the tales.

Among such cues are activities performed or mentioned by the animal characters but associated only with humans in life, so differing from the actions which must be common to men and beasts. We do not, for example think that the country mouse is acting in an unnaturally human fashion because she lives in "ane semple wane" (197), since all must seek shelter, although the standards of men are applied to her dwelling when its lack of fire and candles is noted (202); but her sister's status as "ane fre burges" (172), an entirely human distinction, pokes fun at people of this kind. Similar cues are laughter, kneeling and Christian religious observances, prayers and sacraments. (We could also consider the effects of such institutions as table manners, the use of formal and familiar forms of address and the legal and royal courts.) In speaking of these characteristics, I shall refer particularly to the way the fox uses them. He is the most proficient of all the wrongdoers of the *Fables*, and most villainous when his actions are most human.

As we read we may feel that we share the laughter of members of the audience. More surprisingly, the animal characters also laugh, conspicuously unnatural behaviour which can alert us to expect more dramatic action, usually involving deception and harsh reversal of fortune, generally for the one who laughs. The first creatures to laugh are the two mice, as they embrace at their meeting, "quhylis thay leuch, and quhylis for ioy thay gret, / Quhyle kissit sweit, quhylis in armis plet" (193–194). This laughter occurs in one of the most charming scenes of the *Fables*, one of unalloyed happiness; but we find that the mood can be changed abruptly, as if by a capricious turn of Fortune's wheel, with which the "quhylis ... quhylis" construction becomes associated. Chantecleir's merriment comes after Lowrence's ironically dangerous greeting, telling of the acquaintance with his father, "'Knew ȝe my father?' quod the cok, and leuch" (446). This relaxed moment precedes the flattery which allows Lowrence to snap his jaws on Chantecleir's neck in the way of a natural fox, hoping to hold the son's head, just as he had held the father's. When the cock escapes, the Narrator remarks slyly, "Now iuge ȝe all quhairat schir Lowrence lewch" (571).

The first appearance of the wolf reveals his susceptibility to Lowrence's smooth tongue. When he is asked to hear the fox's confession, "'A, selie Lowrence,' quod the volf, and leuch, / 'It plesis me that ȝe ar penitent'" (684–685). The wolf is further deceived in the next fable, "The Trial of the Fox," when Lowrence persuades him to read the respite written on the mare's hoof. His bloodied scalp causes great amusement at the court of the lion, and the assembled company laughs at the "new-maid doctour off diuinitie" (1052). In this case misfortune comes to Lowrence, and the wolf hears his confession before he is hanged.

Laughter in the later fables is less joyful, being associated with transient or malicious mirth, and with disaster for innocents as well as to malefactors. The foolish lark of "The Preaching of the Swallow" laughs twice at the words of the swallow (1741, 1762), and dies because she fails to heed the warning. In "The Fox, the Wolf, and the Cadger," Lowrence watches the spectacle of the cadger beating the wolf, "And leuch onloft quhen he the volff sa seis" (2187). He laughs again in "The Fox, the Wolf, and the Husbandman:" first when he sees a way to gull the wolf into claiming the oxen (2248), later when he announces that he will be judge in the matter between his dupe and the husbandman (2329) and, after deluding both parties, "[h]alff in to heithing" (2345). When he finds yet another wile, that of the great cheese, he merely smiles softly to himself (2382).

Animals on their knees are rarely showing respect, although all must acknowledge the king of the beasts, and "[b]efoir thair lord the lyoun thay loutit law" (921). Homage to the lion is an act of genuine deference, per-formed in human style in the parody of a royal court, perhaps intended to encourage loyalty to the crown. In "The Trial of the Fox," the Narrator describes the animals as prostrated before their king, "flatlingis to his feit" (924). The fox and wolf kneel before him after their dealings with the mare (1049), and the ewe falls "[b]efoir the iustice on hir kneis" (1069), pleading for lawful vengeance after the taking of her lamb. When he upbraids the mouse in his paw, the lion demands reverence, insisting that even before his skin, "stoppit full of stra" (1450), "[t]how suld for feir on kneis haue fallin doun" (1453).

The fox is a proficient exponent of the human action of kneeling, and he uses it deceitfully, as in his servile greeting to Chantecleir (433); he has no success in his second attempt to entice the cock, when he kneels under the tree to which Chantecleir has flown (572). Freir Volff Waitskaith takes the fox's kneeling as a sign of repentance (671), and, delighted by flattery, agrees to hear Lowrence's confession, saying "sit doun vpon thy kne" (691). This fox's son falls to his knees to give thanks (813), having found his father's body, "nakit, new slane" (812). Deceptive deference is again shown to the wolf in "The Fox, the Wolf, and the Cadger," when the fox gives an apparently respectful greeting, "with ane bek" (1961). Lowrence can persuade the wolf of the need to deceive the cadger to gain his fish, because "He will not giff vs ane hering off his creill, / Befoir ȝone churle on kneis thocht we wald kneill" (2038–2039). The last creature seen on his knees is the luckless wolf, brutally beaten by the cadger and observed by the gleeful fox, "[b]aith deif and dosinnit, fall swonand on his kneis" (2188).

Religious allusions and observances garnish the speech and actions of the characters, placing them in their society and frequently offering sharp comment on the laity and clergy through misunderstood and meaningless ritual and parodies of sacraments. Most of the exclamations and mild oaths are used to add detail to the characterization of the people represented, as may be seen in "The Two Mice." The town mouse's scathing comment on her sister's simple meal is "My Gude Friday is better nor ȝour Pace" (248); and, at the feast she presents, the sisters cry "Haill, ȝule, haill!" (289) in their merriment, although they omit a prayer before, "[w]ithowtin grace, thay wesche and went to meit" (268). The feast is interrupted twice: first by the spenser, when the country mouse cries her preference for the fast of Lent (320–322) and later when the cat comes to bid "God speid" (327). Similar allusions ornament the speech of other characters, for example Sprutok's emphatic "I find Sanct Iohne to borrow" (511), and they are exploited by some.

The fox's approach to spiritual life is his usual one of opportunism. The religious references which decorate his speeches mock those whose words he satirizes and those who accept them. He ingratiates himself with Chantecleir with the assurance that he has said the "Dirigie" over the cock's dead father (449), although a grace might have been more appropriate, and protests the warmth of his feelings "be my saull, and the blissit sacrament" (455). For his jugglings with the sacraments, described so amusingly, he is harshly punished in the tales and vilified in the *moralitates*. We may think of the uncontrite confession which leads to the further crime of renaming the drowned kid in a parody of baptism, important events of "The Fox and the Wolf." In "The Trial of the Fox" which follows, the Narrator speaks ironically of the fox's "naturall pietie" (824), after telling of the jaunty thanksgiving for his inheritance and hasty disposal of his father's body. This fable proves to be another concerned with religious duties, having a sombre *moralitas* which identifies the fox as temptation, and finds, in the incident of the mare's kick, approval for the "men of contemplatioun" (1111) who shun the world. The wolf, whose bleeding scalp earns the title "doctour off diuinitie," hears the fox's confession before the latter's execution, but is shown to be sensuality.

Lowrence is at his most artful when dealing with the wolf, as we see in the two fox and wolf fables which follow "The Preaching of the Swallow." Since the diet of the animals must conform to the church seasons, the fox can offer the obligation to fast during Lent, as a way to persuade his dupe to seek the "nek-hering" through the pretence of death, suggesting as a finishing touch, "I sall say *In principio* vpon ȝow, / And crose ȝour corps from the top to tay" (2154–2155). This trickery fits with Lowrence's oath, sworn by Jupiter and in the ambiguous form, "I sall be treu to ȝou quhill I be deid" (2027), an oath like the one sworn on the fox's tail when he acts as judge, in the dispute between the wolf and the husbandman (2313–2314), and anticipating the toad's oath (2869–2871). The most brazen of Lowrence's religious references, "God is gane to sleip" (2332), spoken as he gives his judgement, recalls the psalm which inspires the sheep's tragic prayer (Psalm 44).

The significance of the use of the religious references is variable. Sprutok's exclamation merely adds another detail to the picture of the character she represents. Some dealings, such as those between the fox and wolf and later between the toad and mouse, satirize ignorance, corruption and unscrupulous reasoning in clergy and laity, but the strongest condemnation is given to those who abuse the sacraments. The fox's adventures have already been mentioned, and the most gruesome case is that of the death of the lamb in "The Wolf and the Lamb." Of all the creatures of the *Fables*, the lamb is the one bearing the heaviest burden of symbolism in Christian tradition. His death is described with grim and potent images, the most impressive being that of a travesty of the eucharist:

> the volff wald do na grace;
> Syne drank his blude and off his flesche can eit
> Quhill he wes full; syne went his way on pace.   (2701–2703)

Emphasizing his horror, the Narrator concludes the tale with a direct comment, "Off his murther quhat sall we say, allace?" (2704), an occurrence which is rare at this stage of the fable cycle. The *moralitas* which follows is the most bitter and detailed of all, and the one most specifically set in the Narrator's time and place, having almost exclusively contemporary relevance in its condemnation of wolves of three kinds who exploit the helpless poor, although its principles could be applied to any age. Although both wrongdoers, the fox and the wolf, provoke the Narrator's anger, only the fox suffers punishment for his blasphemies. It is part of the lamb's tragedy that the wolf leaves the scene of his crime in peace, and with as much authority as he had before.

These cues of conspicuously and exclusively human behaviour alert the audience to expect events which follow almost inevitably. Those who laugh are deceived and in danger. Those who kneel are rarely expressing respect; and religious references often precede satire or direct condemnation. Such sequences are a part of the Narrator's manipulation of his audience, and add to the reader's illusion of joining other listeners, attending to a speaking voice and willingly accepting the notion of truth for the audience from the fiction of the tale.

IV
Truth and the Narrator

The Narrator's first words are concerned with truth and falsehood.
When he tells us

Thocht fein3eit fabils of ald poetre
Be not al grunded vpon truth, 3it than,
Thair polite termes of sweit rhetore
Richt plesand ar vnto the eir of man   (1–4)

he is summarizing a debate which had engaged many medieval scholars.
The patent fiction of fables was condemned by those who advocated moral
instruction in undiluted form, but regarded more tolerantly by those who
approved of their power to attract and refresh the mind: in the Narrator's
words, "to blyth the spreit" (21). Those who saw a benefit in fables also
considered the stories too preposterous to be misleading. The improbable nature of the fabulous animal tales preserved the distinction between
historia, which might be believed, and *fabula*, which clearly should not
(Lenaghan, 1963: 304). We can see that Henryson, speaking through his
Narrator, is one who approves of the fable as a means of enjoyment as
well as moral teaching, an idea borne out in the first few stanzas of "The
Prologue." His choice of metaphors suggests that he is familiar with various
schools of thought, following that of John of Capua in using the figure of the
nutshell and kernel and that of Anthony in his comments on the bent bow.[1]
In its title, the *Moral Fables* promises both instruction and amusement; and
"The Prologue" gives the Narrator's endorsement of the combination. We
may look more closely at the attitudes to truth and falsehood implied by
the Narrator during the *Fables*, and consider how flexibly he regards these
absolutes when he deals ironically with deception and candour.

In a work of moral instruction we may expect the praise of truth and
condemnation of falsehood to be unequivocal, and the tales to illustrate
known and perhaps proverbial maxims. Indeed, fables may be expected
often to be expanded proverbs. Villains should be clearly villains and those
who speak the truth should be obviously good characters. The earliest

---

[1] The sources of these images are given by Glending Olson (Olson, 1974: 296, 303).
The issues of truth in fables and the medieval acceptance of this possibility have been
extensively investigated, and Olson and Stephen Manning (Manning, 1960) give detailed
accounts of the views of these authorities and others such as Augustine, Isidore of Seville,
Conrad of Hirschau, Bonaventura and Hugh of St Victor.

fables and *exempla* were not intended to be works of great subtlety. How disconcerting then to find in Henryson's *Fables* that true words are often put into the mouths of rogues, proverbs are contradicted, sometimes with other proverbs, and obvious morals are ignored in favour of obscure and surprising ones. This is not to say that rogues are not condemned and the truth not shown as an ideal, as in the Narrator's exclamation, "fle the filth of falset, I the reid" (983); but in the *Fables*, as in life, praise and apparent success are not confined to those who merit them and truth may be manipulated. We may also find one rogue among the most engaging in the cast of characters. How then should we regard the true statements placed in the mouths of characters who are clearly introduced to be condemned? Their speakers must detract from their worth and make us suspicious even of the truth. Many statements must be deflated or discounted, if only because they have been made by such characters as the fox and wolf, eventually casting doubt on many of the principles held in everyday life.

Let us consider the case of the obviously villainous Lowrence, the fox. The Narrator prepares the way for him in the list of natural characteristics of creatures in the opening stanza of "The Cock and the Fox," "the fox fenȝeit, craftie and cawtelous" (402). These adjectives, with a few others, are repeated frequently and become associated with the fox. He is "this wylie tod" (425), "fenȝeit foxe, fals and dissimulate" (460), "fals and friuolus" (565) and later "this wylie tratour tod" (670). "Fenȝeit" gains an association beyond its first use to describe fables, and when the Narrator speaks of "[t]his foirsaid foxe" (796), the thoughts which come to the audience must be of Lowrence's wicked cunning. Descriptive details such as his sharp grey eyes and red coat are superfluous, and remain unmentioned because they are unimportant in the early tales. Lowrence himself speaks of his appearance only when he is trying to avoid serving the wolf as a steward in "The Fox, the Wolf, and the Cadger" (1976, 1991), and as a part of his deception. The fox's knavery is beyond any doubt, yet this wickedness is offset when he is introduced in "The Cock and the Fox." He is "[f]ull sair hungrie" (426) when he lies in wait for Chantecleir. A fox's wiliness is not only natural but essential, and Lowrence is always an amusing exponent of his gift.

The deception of Chantecleir which follows is a delightfully ironic scene. Lowrence manipulates the truth outrageously, but an examination of his artful speeches reveals a surprising number of true statements. He assures the cock that he has come to serve him, that he had known his father, and was with the elder bird when he died, devotedly holding his head, that he would creep on his belly after Chantecleir in the harshest weather, that the sight of him warms his heart. Chantecleir is so willing to be flattered that his own foolishness accomplishes most of his undoing. The fox's truth is the ironic, misleading kind found in messages from oracles. Who could doubt that Lowrence had known Chantecleir's father, who had provided food, had held his head when he died, and would slink after Chantecleir, anxious to serve him in the same way? Who but Chantecleir would laugh delightedly at such news and easily believe that his song could be made yet sweeter, as sweet as his father's, if only he would close his eyes and turn himself around? This episode shows that the truth can be just as cloudy and deceiving as falsehood when it is manipulated by a devious character. The flatterer himself is later outwitted by his victim's use of deception, when Chantecleir persuades Lowrence to turn and speak to his pursuers. The Narrator tells us that "falset failȝeis ay at the latter end" (568), but the story shows that falsehood, judiciously mingled with truth, can have some temporary success. Later he shows disturbing examples of the triumph of fraud and injustice over defenceless victims who trust in the power of the truth.

In "The Fox and the Wolf," Lowrence again speaks the truth, and more of it than he knows. He is certainly near to danger when he casts his horoscope, and the precaution of confessing his sins is an inspired piece of jiggery-pokery. Death for him will be the "reward off sin and schamefull end" (653), but his show of regret for the life of a thief is short-lived and preposterous:

'Allace . . . richt waryit ar we theuis:
Our lyif is set ilk nicht in auenture,
Our cursit craft full mony man mischeuis,
For euer we steill and euer alyk ar pure;
In dreid and schame our dayis we indure,
Syne "Widdinek" and "Craikraip" callit als,
And till our hyre ar hangit be the hals.'   (656–662)

This remorse is only temporary, and in his dealings with the wolf we see Lowrence's old spirit, expressed in his exaggerated respect for Freir Volff Waitskaith and the brazen frankness of his confession. Here we may gratefully note that the Narrator does not tell the truth when he tells us that he will withdraw from this sacramental scene:

Quhen I this saw, I drew ane lytill by,
For it effeiris nouther to heir nor spy
Nor to reueill thing said vnder that seill.   (694–696)

Fortunately he gives us all the details.

As confessions go it is unsatisfactory, but Lowrence is surely being quite candid when he denies any feeling of contrition about the life he had professed to regret when his confessor asks if he repents:

> 'Na, schir, I can not duid.
> Me think that hennis ar sa honie sweit,
> And lambes flesche that new ar lettin bluid,
> For to repent my mynd can not concluid,
> Bot off this thing, that I haif slane sa few.'   (699–703)

He is open, too, when he denies the possibility of amending his wicked life;
but his reason, need, could be sustained only to such a confessor, and the
exchange must be considered an anti-clerical jibe, an example of *confessio
Reynardi* (Friedman, 1967). The fox's plea,

> 'And I forbeir, how sall I leif, allace,
> Haifand nane vther craft me to defend?
> Neid causis me to steill quhair euer I wend:
> I eschame to thig, I can not wirk, ʒe wait,
> ʒit wald I fane pretend to gentill stait'   (707–711)

and his talk of sickliness—he is "baith lene and sklender" (718), in perfect
hunting trim—gain him concessions in his penance of fasting, "for neid may
haif na law" (731). Both fox and wolf interpret this proverb as it suits them,
and Lowrence's light-hearted attempt at penance leads to his most blatant
abuse of the truth, a parody of the sacrament of baptism, when he drowns
a kid and names it salmon before eating it. Justice overtakes Lowrence,
just as he had foretold that it would, and his unrepentant, though truthful,
confession gives no protection against the goatherd's arrow. His last words
are a rueful comment on his fate and truth: "Me think na man may speik
ane word in play, / Bot now on dayis in ernist it is tane" (770–771). In
natural terms the fox's hunting can be justified, and should cause no guilt,
since no other life could sustain him; but Lowrence represents those human
beings who prey on others when they could find an alternative, and the
fabulist artfully blends animal and human nature.

We do not expect honesty from a character like the fox, and look forward
to his crafty and outrageous manipulation of the truth, enjoying the effects,
particularly on the other archvillain of the *Fables*, the wolf. The wolf is a
rogue of an entirely different kind: brutal, stupid, vicious and often the victim of the fox. We feel no pity when he is deceived and are amused by such
savage consequences as the mare's kick and the cadger's beating. It is surprising to find that he also often speaks the truth, and in its most accepted
and recognized form, that of proverbs. Regrettably, they are often shown
to be misapplied by a mind lacking in originality and perception. "Neid
may haif na law" is proverbial and a useful justification for the misdeeds of
a villain who would sin in any case, but as spiritual advice it is superficial
and venal. The wolf uses many proverbs in "The Fox, the Wolf, and the

Cadger" when he tries to bully the fox to become his steward, including even the warning given by the Narrator, "Falset will failȝe ay at the latter end" (1997). Ironically, he takes no warning from this nor from another proverb used to encourage Lowrence: "For euerie wrink, forsuith, thow hes ane wyle" (1987). The advice might have been invaluable, but he cannot realize that, for him, it is pointless to try to use Lowrence's methods on the fox himself. Lowrence tricks him into dangerously unnatural behaviour, just as he tricked Chantecleir, by giving his victim welcome news. He tells the wolf that the infuriated cadger wants to give a "nekhering," quite true, then invents the enticing fiction of just what this means—an enormous fish rather than a vicious blow.[2]

A more vulnerable subject, the husbandman of "The Fox, the Wolf, and the Husbandman," can be overwhelmed by a barrage of proverbs combined with his powerful fear of the fox and wolf. When the wolf claims the husbandman's oxen, after the man's reckless cursing of the fractious beasts—"The volff ... mot haue ȝou all at anis!" (2244)—he strengthens his specious argument with the saws:

'is thair oucht, sayis thou, frear than gift?'   (2268)

'Far better is frelie for to giff ane plank
Nor be compellit on force to giff ane mart.'   (2270–2271)

'ane lord, and he be leill,
That schrinkis for schame, or doutis to be repruuit—
His sau is ay als sickker as his seill.'   (2280–2282)

'For it is said in prouerb: "But lawte
All vther vertewis ar nocht worth ane fle." '   (2285–2286)

The wolf's unscrupulous use of the accepted truths of these proverbs gives a pretence of legitimacy to his unjustified and extortionate demand for the cattle; the second is no more than a threat issued in proverbial style. The one proverb used in the husbandman's obviously reasonable reply is simply outnumbered. "Ane leill man is not tane at halff a taill" (2288) is sufficient in quality but not in quantity. In this case, only dishonest means, the bribery of a false judge, will gain a just judgement; and Lowrence too, the "iuge amycabill" (2310), uses proverbial sayings when he puts his unjustifiable case:

'Seis thou not buddis beiris bernis throw,
And giftis garris crukit materis hald full euin?

---

[2] Lyall comments on the fox's obvious familiarity with this unusual word (Lyall 1985: 18–19), disgreeing with Fox's suggestion that Lowrence may not understand it (Fox, 1981: 294–295).

Sumtymis ane hen haldis ane man in ane kow;
All ar not halie that heifis thair handis to heuin.'

(2322–2325)

The discrediting of proverbs which occurs in "The Preaching of the Swallow" is more disturbing than the examples mentioned above, because in this tale the proverbs are used in good faith, by characters who trust in their wisdom. As in the fox and wolf fables, they are used to contradict one another, and the proverbs which should not be heeded prevail because they are more numerous and so appear more convincing. The swallow's warning to the other birds, eventually so brutally vindicated, is backed by only one proverb, "It is grit wisedome to prouyde befoir" (1739), and its Latin equivalent, "*Nam leuius laedit quicquid praeuidimus ante*" (1754). Her preaching is brief, wise and cogent, but its proverbial content is simply outweighed by the jumble of old sayings produced by the chattering lark:

The lark, lauchand, the swallow thus couth scorne,
And said scho fischit lang befoir the net—
'The barne is eith to busk that is vnborne;
All growis nocht that in the ground is set;
The nek to stoup quhen it the straik sall get
Is sone aneuch; deith on the fayest fall.'   (1762–1767)

The light-hearted bird gives cheering, welcome news, which is, unintentionally, as deceptive as any given by the fox. Her misinterpreted proverbs appear to be more specific in their application than the swallow's, with the garbled talk of nets and crops which might not grow. In fact the lark's proverbs are disastrously appropriate, since many birds do lose their heads and most are fated to die at the fowler's hands, trapped in the nets he spreads on the ground. The lark, like Lowrence when he reads the stars, speaks more truth than she knows, and does not understand its implications.

There are similar exchanges of conventional wisdom in "The Paddock and the Mouse." Here the mouse realizes that she should mistrust the toad, because an evil nature is revealed by the creature's ugly appearance. She can cite authorities and a proverb to support her case:

'For clerkis sayis the inclinatioun
Off mannis thocht proceidis commouly
Efter the corporall complexioun
To gude and euill, as nature will apply:
Ane thrawart will, ane thrawin phisnomy.
The auld prouerb is witnes off this *lorum*:
Distortum vultum sequitur distortio morum.'   (2826–2832)

The toad outwits her with a much longer argument, by appealing to apparently plausible common sense, talking of bilberries, less attractive but more useful than primroses, and of her inability to control her appearance. For authorities she appeals to scripture, referring to the beauty of "iolie Absolon" (2842), and to more proverbs, even one which brazenly admits that a "silkin toung" (2848) may exist with a "mynd inconstant, false, and wariand, / Full off desait and menis cautelous" (2849-2850). She is a frightening example.

We may wonder why such sayings, long established and accepted as truth, should be shown as contradictory and apparently worthless. Even proverbs which have a value are not recognized as applying to the situation in which their users find themselves. Yet the tale of a fable has often been an illustration of a proverb, with the proverb itself as the moral. The Narrator's style discredits accepted, unquestioned maxims as a collection of equal and opposite old saws of doubtful value, which may mislead as often as they teach, and shows the folly of unthinking reliance on them. And just as proverbs may not be invariably useful, so the words of villains may not be false. How then does the Narrator regard the truth? He begins the *Moral Fables* by speaking of the truth to be found in fables, the justification for their existence, but gives a contradictory picture as he continues. We see that the truth can be manipulated by rogues and accepted by the gullible as having the meaning they wish to hear, and that some characters speak the truth in ways they do not realize.

How does the Narrator speak the truth to his audience? We may accept that he tells it without disguise in the *moralitates*, but truth in the tales may be ironic or even frankly misleading. We need not take seriously such lines as those which introduce

Ane worthie doctour of diuinitie,
Freir Volff Waitskaith, in science wonder sle,
To preiche and pray ... new cum from the closter,
With beidis in hand, sayand his Pater Noster   (666-669)

and we are not likely to be misled by a description of this kind. On the other hand we may understand the thoughts and misguided good intentions of such characters as the cock who rejected the jasp or the wether who disguised himself as a sheepdog, so that the judgements delivered on them in the *moralitates* of "The Cock and the Jasp" and "The Wolf and the Wether" can seem unexpectedly and unreasonably harsh, making the tales seem just such a manipulation of the truth as we see in the mouths of rogues.

The tales of sheep and their dealings with the truth give an increasingly sad commentary on the wisdom of relying on the truth. A ewe complains at the court of the lion that the fox has taken her lamb, in "The Trial of the Fox." In this just court, Lowrence's excuse, "My purpois wes with him to haif plaid" (1079), is quickly shown to be false when the ewe gives gruesome proof:

'Thow leis,' quod scho, 'fals tyke!
'His deith be practik may be preuit eith:
Thy gorrie gumis and thy bludie snout;
The woll, the flesche, ȝit stikkis on thy teith;
And that is euidence aneuch, but dout.'   (1082–1086)

The fox is punished in formal, judicial style, making a last confession to the wolf before being hanged by the ape. Thus the ewe's plea in a court of justice is a happy example of the triumph of truth over base falsehood, a sufficient defence against injustice. It is regrettable that the other sheep of the *Fables* do not know such success.

The unfortunate sheep of "The Sheep and the Dog" gains no justice when he truthfully denies not only the false charge brought by the dog but also the jurisdiction of the court itself. This court is sitting at an unlawful time and place and is filled with officials known to prey on sheep, such as the raven, fox and kite, with the judge, "[a]ne fraudfull volff" (1150), declaring himself "partles off fraud and gyle" (1155). How could the sheep hope for justice in spite of the truth of his pleas? The proceedings of the court are at first recounted in ironic style, with the futile activity of the bear and badger held to be that of "trew iugis. I schrew thame ay that leis" (1222). When these creatures find that the sheep must still answer the case, with no appeal against the sentence, the Narrator speaks more clearly: "On clerkis I do it, gif this sentence wes leill" (1229). "Fals" is the adjective he employs to describe the dog's case (1180), the dog himself (1243), the means used against helpless people (1261) and the fox (1279). From such a court only a false judgement could be expected, and the sheep loses his fleece to pay the dog five shillings for a loaf of bread. As he mourns in a cave, sheltering from the bleak winter weather, we may wonder if he will also lose his life. He must, in any case, pay dearly for trusting in the truth of his case in a corrupt court of law. "The Wolf and the Wether" tells a story which seems to show that one cannot even rely on the defence of falsehood, since the wether, trying to disguise himself as a sheepdog, although for an apparently good reason, is viciously killed by the wolf he has terrified.

The contrast in strength between victim and predator increases in scale as the series proceeds, emphasizing the magnitude of the injustice done to those whose only defence can be the truth of their cause. In the last of the sheep fables, "The Wolf and the Lamb," the protagonists are the most helpless victim and the most vicious predator. This fable is the only one in the cycle which is told almost without humour. (Even "The Sheep and the Dog" has the irony of the grotesquely unsuitable court officials.) The tale tells of a lamb, pleading for the justice of a court where he may defend himself against the wolf's charge that he is polluting and poisoning the water where they drink, and the telling stresses the differences between the creatures. The wolf's accusations and threats are brutal and clearly false, as the lamb can show. He pleads his case eloquently and reasonably and asks to be taken before "ane lauchfull court" (2686); but the wolf's reply is that of a tyrant:

'Ha ... thou wald intruse ressoun
Quhair wrang and reif suld duell in propertie.
That is ane poynt and part of fals tressoun,
For to gar reuth remane with crueltie.' (2693–2696)

Although the lamb's defence is ordered, reasonable and true, he is denied justice; having no other defence against the brutal wolf, he loses his life. It is disquieting to see that even in the artificial, idealized world of fables the truth may not be enough, and that injustice may prevail even when true words are spoken against it. "The Sheep and the Dog" and "The Wolf and the Lamb" give the lie to "falset failʒeis ay at the latter end," and "The Wolf and the Wether" shows that even deception may not help the weak. We can gain little comfort from the stories of sheep.

The *Fables* show us that life may be more difficult and need more thought than we at first suppose. Henryson's Narrator's idea that truth may be insufficient and manipulated by the wicked is a part of his outlook on life, an outlook which seems cynical at times but is always undeceived. He is showing us an imperfect world in a mirror which sometimes exaggerates but does not distort beyond recognition. The world created in Henryson's *Fables* is an absurdly preposterous one, yet it gives penetrating insights into the world of human beings, never more so than in its dealings with the truth.

V
The *moralitates* of the *Fables*

The Narrator concludes the first *moralitas*, that of "The Cock and the Jasp," with the command, "Ga seik the jasp, quha will" (161). The jasp is the precious gift of wisdom which could help man to the ideal life, "now, allace, ... tynt and hid" (155), as was the importance of the stone found by the cock. As this was hidden from him so may be the significance of the tales, and one of the Narrator's tasks is to show his audience how to appreciate the moral lessons of his fables. The cock sees the obvious and superficial attributes of the jasp, and man may be trusted to see the obvious morals of the *Fables*, but he needs more instruction to find "science"— their deeper, hidden implications. It is useful to examine the *moralitates* themselves to see how they teach and progress to show an audience not only the moral of each fable but also the way to apprehend such lessons, and find the unifying strands of moral teaching which run through the fable cycle.

A brief survey of critical comments on the *moralitates* reveals some variation in attitudes towards them in the twentieth century, although it seems unlikely that their presence would have caused any surprise when the *Fables* were written. They are, after all, *moral* fables, and this title clearly implies instruction as well as entertainment. It would probably surprise the original audience to know that the *moralitates* were later regarded as boring and unnecessary, no more than annoying impediments to the enjoyment of the tales, with descriptions such as Kinsley's relatively mild "often too ingenious for modern taste" (Kinsley, 1955: 18), and Wood's comment that "the moralising, which is admittedly dull, is confined to the postscript" (Wood, 1958: xv). Perhaps the most damning judgement is given by Burrow, who writes that "most present-day readers of Henryson's Fables find his Moralitates at best unpleasing and at worst desperately confusing" (Burrow, 1975: 35). Since the moralizing is by no means confined to the postscripts to the tales, those with no taste for it may well find much of the work dull. It is not possible, however, to dismiss the moralizing postscripts without maiming the fables. In Fox's words, "the *moralitas* is never an arbitrary appendage" (Fox, 1962: 348). Without an explanation, the antics of the beasts in the tales would have little purpose, a point taken up by Carens, who summarizes the complementary nature of the tale and *moralitas* as follows:

38

> One might almost say that without the morality there would
> be no fun: if life is meaningless and absurd, if men are to be
> left to their own devices in a godless universe, what possible
> reason can a man find to be amused by his own carnal nature?
> (Carens, 1974: 81)

In the series of *moralitates* the audience moves through stages of manipulation by the Narrator. First come the surprises of the *moralitas* of "The Cock and the Jasp," which show the need for the Narrator's guidance. Then the straightforward moral of "The Two Mice" gives confidence, and the *moralitas* of "The Cock and the Fox" continues the pedagogic style of its tale in setting the allegory as an exercise in deduction. *Moralitates* which follow leave members of the audience free to add their own thoughts, but the Narrator expresses his interpretations unequivocally, frequently adding material which is not obvious in the tales, leaving the more salient lessons to his audience. The *moralitates* offer then, as well as moral instruction, a course in finding moral instruction, designed to take each member of the audience from the status of beginner to a standard of proficiency, in "The Paddock and the Mouse," surpassed only by that of the friars, whose ingenuity in finding morals was notorious. Let us examine this progression and its implications.[1]

The first moral has already been described in some detail. It is a part of Henryson's introduction of his Narrator, a learning process which confuses and surprises his audience, and may even exasperate them, but must lead to dependence on his comments. The tale of "The Cock and the Jasp" may evoke sympathy for the imperceptive creature, but the moral deals with him harshly, deriding his illusion of knowledge and self-sufficiency, and showing his inadequacy, when he rejects the jasp which could bring wisdom, courage and success in enterprise. For one who could find it and appreciate it, there would be no need for more teaching, but the *Fables* are designed for imperfect man, and so there are more lessons to be taught and learned.

After a difficult lesson, the Narrator chooses one which seems reassuringly straightforward. From "The Two Mice" he selects the need for contentment with one's lot as his theme in the *moralitas*. This moral is the most obvious one in the fable cycle, and differs from the others (apart from a section of "The Paddock and the Mouse"), in the style of its expression, in stanzas of eight-line ballade form, each with a rigidly repetitive rhyme scheme and ending with a line about "small possessioun" which forms a

---

[1] The complementary effect of the reader's education is described by Evelyn S. Newlyn, who refers to "The Cock and the Jasp," "The Wolf and the Wether" and "The Paddock and the Mouse" (Newlyn, 1982).

chorus. The song-like character and intimate manner of address are unlike the didactic hectoring found in "The Cock and the Jasp." The Narrator's manner is more gentle, beginning "Freindis, heir may ʒe find, will ʒe tak heid, / In this fabill ane gude moralitie" (365–366), implying the audience's willing engagement with the easy task of discerning the moral message in the tale. His imagery is familiar and concrete, proceeding from particular example to general application, as in the figure,

> As fitchis myngit ar with nobill seid,
> Swa intermellit is aduersitie
> With eirdlie ioy.   (367–369)

The benefits of contentment are expressed positively in biblical and proverbial fashion:

> Blissed be sempill lyfe withoutin dreid;
> Blissed be sober feist in quietie.
> Quha has aneuch, of na mair hes he neid.
> Thocht it be littill into quantatie   (373–376)

with the sternest warning given to "wantoun man that vsis for to feid / Thy wambe, and makis it a god to be" (381–382)—the threat that "The cat cummis and to the mous hes ee" (384). The scale of this *moralitas* seems smaller than that of "The Cock and the Jasp." Its message is not to go out and seek the unattainable perfection symbolized by the jasp, but rather to remain content with "small possessioun," expressed as "Thy awin fyre, freind, thocht it be bot ane gleid" (389). The effect is of comforting anticlimax, after the ambitious counsels of the first *moralitas*. It seems to bring the ideal life and perceptions of wisdom within reach, and apparently contradicts the moral of "The Cock and the Jasp." This last consideration is masked by the separation of the two *moralitates* by the engaging tale of "The Two Mice," and the audience may move with confidence to the next part of the instruction.

The telling of the tale of "The Cock and the Fox" at times suggests the schoolroom and the *moralitas* continues to give this impression.[2] The Narrator has bullied and confused, then given a straightforward example in the previous *moralitates*; now the audience must begin to work, being urged to consider the tale as a fable containing a message, just as school pupils might be addressed. Stages in the exposition are introduced with tentative and encouraging phrases—"Now worthie folk, suppose this be ane fabill" (586), going on to suggest "ʒit may ʒe find ane sentence richt

---

[2] I.R. Carruthers notes the resemblance of the opening stanzas of the tale to Aristotle's classification of animals in *Historia Animalium* (Carruthers, 1978: 278–279).

agreabill" (588), including the Narrator himself in "To our purpose this cock weill may we call / Nyse proud men" (590–591). This exposition is set out as an exploration of allegory, but there is nothing tentative in the condemnation of the vices of pride and flattery when their perpetrators have been identified. Although he seems to guide the audience diffidently through this identification, the Narrator leaves no doubt about the message of the *moralitas*: "Thir twa sinnis, flatterie and vaneglore, / Ar vennomous: gude folk, fle thame thairfoir!" (612–613).

The vigorously didactic style of this conclusion continues in the *moralitas* of "The Fox and the Wolf" which follows. It also shows the characteristic style of the Narrator in singling out one message among several which could compete for the audience's attention. There is no talk of specific vices symbolized by the beasts of the tale, although we realize that both fox and wolf are juggling with the truth and represent hypocrites of the laity and clergy; Lowrence is also dabbling in astrology. The short *moralitas* concentrates on just one example of neglect of Christian duty—imperfect penitence—giving no further attention to the corrupt friar to whom exaggerated and obviously insincere respect is given, the haggling over the penance and the parody of baptism to dodge it. These discoveries are left to the audience. This *moralitas* is the most alarming so far delivered. That of "The Two Mice" implies a threat in the line, "The cat cummis and to the mous hes ee" (384); but the mouse escapes danger, and the effect is not disturbing. Similarly, we do not fear for the life of proud Chantecleir in "The Cock and the Fox," probably because the loss of the human victim represented by the cock would be that of riches or reputation, and the villain the fox portrays is a swindler, not a murderer.

The moral of "The Fox and the Wolf" is the first to emphasize the terror of sudden death. As well as the familiar threats of plague and war, there were literary reminders of this horror to an audience of Henryson's era, from the genre of *memento mori*, including two of Henryson's other works, "The Ressoning betuix Deth and Man" and "The Thre Deid Pollis," and this *moralitas*, although it comes after a lightheartedly satirical tale, serves the same purpose of warning the listeners that only a soul prepared for death can face it with diminished fear. Death comes to the fox as rough justice in this tale and in formally judicial fashion in "The Trial of Fox" which follows, and is grimly personified as the vicious cadger of "The Fox, the Wolf, and the Cadger." Only in the *moralitates* of "The Fox and the Wolf" and "The Trial of the Fox" can we find any defence against the universal and inevitable end, when the Narrator warns against the imperfect preparation of unrepentant confession, and, in "The Trial of the Fox," shows that the mare's hoof represents the salutary thought of death which can overcome sensuality. The Narrator's stress on the need for contrite confession suggests that he considers it too important to be left to the audience and perhaps ignored among other distracting messages. He leaves no room for doubt in the resolute advice which concludes the *moralitas*: "Do wilful pennance here; and ȝe sall wend, / Efter ȝour deith, to blis withouttin end" (794–795), the first message which speaks of the reward of an after-life rather than improvement in man's life on earth.

The first stanza of the *moralitas* of "The Trial of the Fox" reminds the audience of the original style and purpose of the *Fables*. The metaphor of refining gold from base metals,

> Richt as the mynour in his minorall
> Fair gold with fyre may fra the leid weill wyn,
> Richt so vnder ane fabill figurall
> Sad sentence men may seik, and efter fyne,
> As daylie dois the doctouris of deuyne,
> That to our leuing full weill can apply
> And paynt thair mater furth be poetry   (1097–1103)

is reminiscent of the figures of "The Prologue," and anticipates the sheep's reference to a reversal of this process in the *moralitas* of "The Sheep and the Dog." When applied here to the search for a moral, an activity of "the doctouris of deuyne," the allusion is like that of the last stanza of the *Fables*, which concludes the *moralitas* of "The Paddock and the Mouse," and ironically directs all unmentioned morals to the friars. All the teaching of the *moralitas* of "The Trial of the Fox" is concentrated on the last scenes of the tale, and is heavily allegorical, being delivered in the didactic style of the pulpit. It gives a great deal of very specific explanation and suggests interpretations which may not have been obvious even to the original audience. The allegory involves largely abstract entities: the world, sensuality, the thought of death, temptations; even "men of contemplatioun" (1111) is a term used rather vaguely, elaborated as those "[o]ff pennance walkand in this wildernes, / As monkis and othir men of religioun" (1112–1113).

Although the qualities presented are abstract and generally intangible, the teaching is specific and vigorous, and the moral is not left to be drawn out by the audience. It is very detailed and based on a short section of the tale, an incident of heartless and thoughtless amusement, which could be overlooked if the audience paid more attention to apparently more significant or dramatic parts of the tale, such as the procession of the animals or the ewe's plea. The exposition of the allegory is clear, and the Narrator's presence and function as teacher are implicit in the repetitive construction which begins three stanzas of this *moralitas* and is later found in others: "This volf I likkin to sensualitie" (1118), "Hir hufe I likkin to the thocht of deid" (1125), and "This tod I likkin to temptationis" (1132). The warning against sensuality is unequivocal but hopeful:

Fle fast thairfra, gif thow will richt remord.
Than sall ressoun ryse, rax, and ring,
And for thy saull thair is na better thing.   (1122–1124)

Although the Narrator's pedagogic presence is evident, the *moralitas* ends, after a prayer, by giving some credit to the favourite villain of the *Fables*, with the enigmatic line, "And thus endis the talking of the tod" (1145).

The style of the preceding *moralitas* is also that of "The Sheep and the Dog," but the range of the didactic attack is narrowed. Using the "I likkin" device, the Narrator identifies particular wrongdoers among the court officials satirized in the tale. The wolf, for example, is likened to "ane schiref stout" (1265) and the raven to "ane fals crownair" (1272), whose misdeed is precisely described as "To scraip out Iohne, and wryte in Will or Wat" (1277). The *moralitas* has moved from general moral teaching to an exact account of contemporary and familiar corruption, directed towards particular individuals rather than all members of the audience. This *moralitas* differs from all others in continuing the tale it expounds, by including the speech of the shorn sheep, overheard by the Narrator, just as he later overhears the conversations of the birds of "The Preaching of the Swallow." As well as mourning his own wretched circumstances, the sheep refers to the general condition of oppression of the poor, the effect of "this cursit syn of couetice" (1300). In telling of the overturning of order the sheep refers to the refining of gold, but his use of the figure inverts the Narrator's in the previous *moralitas*. The sheep pleads:

'Seis thow not, lord, this warld ouerturnit is,
As quha wald change gude gold in leid or tyn?
The pure is peillit, the lord may do na mis,
And simonie is haldin for na syn.   (1307–1310)

The *moralitas* concludes with a prayer for rest in heaven, as do several others, but the sheep's prayer, beginning "O lord, quhy sleipis thow sa lang?" (1295), resembling Psalm 44, gives no hope of any happiness in life on earth.

Aesop delivers the *moralitas* of "The Lion and the Mouse," just as he tells the tale. It could be thought that the moral is in the last stanza of the tale—

Now is the lyoun fre off all danger,
Lows and delyuerit to his libertie
Be lytill beistis off ane small power,
As ʒe haue hard, because he had pietie   (1566–1569)

—or in the words of the mouse, "For oft is sene, ane man off small stature / Reskewit hes ane lord off hie honour" (1499–1500). We may wonder why the Narrator asks so ostentatiously for a moral to the tale:

> Quod I, 'Maister, is thair ane moralitie
> In this fabill?' '3ea, sone,' he said, 'richt gude.'
> 'I pray 3ow, schir,' quod I, '3e wald conclude.'   (1570–1572)

The audience must appreciate the application of this lesson; and this teaching, which comes from Aesop's remarks on the duties of princes, is perhaps more tactfully and forcefully put into the mouth of a long-dead authority than that of a contemporary narrator, although both are devices of the author. The moral which has already been stated twice is repeated, but Aesop's version carries the hint of a threat:

> Oftymis is sene ane man of small degre
> Hes quit ane commoun, baith for gude and ill,
> As lord hes done rigour or grace him till   (1598–1600)

offset by the suggestion that "fals fortoun" may be responsible for the downfall of "ane lord of grit renoun, / Rolland in wardlie lust and vane plesance" (1601–1602).

These devices may have been intended to avoid giving offence to James III, in whose turbulent reign the poem was probably written, as has been suggested by several critics, but some of the personified explanations of the allegory may seem to be, even more than the *moralitas*, "too ingenious for modern taste."[3] The particular explanations, although they are subtle and apparently plausible, actually take from the fable its most important characteristic, the application to mankind in general, and could reduce it to mere political satire of limited and short-lived application. The warning to an unwise and slothful authority that negligence might lead him into danger could apply to king, emperor, prime minister or president, could extend beyond the political sphere, and is too important and universal to be given only to one individual. Similarly, the "lordis of prudence" (1594), who are urged to consider the "vertew of pietie" (1595), may appear in many forms and places. Only in Henryson's time could one unmask the lion as James III, the hunters as the leaders of the Lauder rebellion and the mice as the burgesses of Edinburgh, and this may well be no more than coincidence.

---

[3] E.g. those given by John MacQueen, R.L. Kindrick and James Kinsley (MacQueen, 1967: 170–173; Kindrick, 1979: 128–131; Kinsley, 1955: 16). Many of the references are summarized and refuted by R.J. Lyall (Lyall, 1976: 7–10). The debate is continued and extended by Kindrick (Kindrick, 1984).

44

Both the tale and moral of this fable are optimistic, allowing the possibility of a prompt reward for a good deed and suggesting that prayers should be offered for peace in the realm, for an improvement in human rather than the hope of heavenly life. It is a sad comment that the *moralitas*, like the tale, is assumed to be a part of the Narrator's dream, and that he now leaves the world of dreams and fables to take his place in the world of men, in an atmosphere of generally increasing pessimism, more often asserting himself in the *moralitates* than in the tales, although his idiosyncratic style continues to assure us of his presence in both.

"The Preaching of the Swallow" resembles "The Lion and the Mouse" in stating its most obvious moral as the tale concludes, when the swallow, assuming the role of "halie preichour" sadly states

'Lo ... thus it happinnis mony syis
On thame that will not tak counsall nor reid
Off prudent men or clerkis that ar wyis.'   (1882–1884)

It may be because of this pessimistic statement and the wish for added authority that the Narrator gives Aesop some credit for the formal *moralitas*, but it is delivered in the Narrator's familiar style, with a detailed exposition identifying the fowler as the devil and describing at length the growth of sin which traps the soul with empty pleasures.[4] As in other *moralitates* we may gain the impression that he does not trust his audience to find every nuance of the allegory and suspects that they may wish to ignore some of them. Indeed it would be difficult to appreciate such specific details as those of the gruesome deaths of the trapped birds, "Off sum the heid, off sum he brak the crag, / Sum half on lyfe he stoppit in his bag" (1879–1890), explained in the rhetoric of the pulpit:

Quhat help is than this calf, thir gudis vane,
Quhen thow art put in Luceferis bag,
And brocht to hell, and hangit be the crag?   (1934–1936)

Since worldly possessions are attractive to many, the Narrator may mention this temptation so that it will not be ignored as was the swallow's preaching.

---

[4] The Narrator associates Aesop with the *moralitas* in its first stanza, although he does not directly suggest that it is Aesop's work, as he does in "The Lion and the Mouse":

Lo, worthie folk, Esope, that nobill clerk,
Ane poet worthie to be lawreate,
Quhen that he waikit from mair authentik werk,
With vther ma, this foirsaid fabill wrate,
Quhilk at this tyme may weill be applicate
To gude morall edificatioun,
Haifand ane sentence according to ressoun.   (1888–1894)

The need to heed warnings is obvious, but unwelcome messages may still be overlooked. In returning to his old style of instruction the Narrator shows that he does not yet trust his "worthie folk" to find all the important teachings of his tales without aid. The *moralitas* repeats an old lesson and hints at others which are to come. The warning of this fable, "Best is bewar in maist prosperitie; / For in this warld thair is na thing lestand" (1939–1940), echoes the lesson of "The Two Mice" and anticipates that of "The Wolf and the Wether." Similarly, the grim description of the separation of soul and body,

> Allace, quhat cair, quhat weiping is and wo,
> Quhen saull and bodie partit ar in twane!
> The bodie to the wormis keitching go,
> The saull to fyre, to euerlastand pane   (1930–1933)

foreshadows in harshest terms the possibilities implied in "The Paddock and the Mouse."

The Narrator's pedagogic style permeates the *moralitates* of the two fables which follow. "The Fox, the Wolf, and the Cadger" and "The Fox, the Wolf, and the Husbandman" are explained in the unequivocal, detailed fashion of the earlier fox and wolf fables—"The Fox and the Wolf" and "The Trial of the Fox." They have compact morals which imply familiarity with the lessons given before; the allegory is concise in style to the point of compression, and is expanded only to give details and emphases not obvious in the tales. For example, the "I likkin" construction is implied but contracted in the three clipped lines which identify the symbolic figures of "The Fox, the Wolf, and the Cadger":

> The foxe vnto the warld may likkinnit be;
> The reuand wolf vnto ane man, but leis;
> The cadgear, deith, quhome vnder all men preis.   (2205–2207)

Expansion of these lines is essential, since the moral implications noted by the Narrator are by no means conspicuous in the tale. They are amplified partly by tacit dependence on earlier teaching, conveyed in "The warld, 3e wait, is stewart to the man" (2210), which assumes the notion of man at the centre of creation, as stated in the prologue of "The Preaching of the Swallow." The tricks of the fox as the world, rather than as a human flatterer are then given more serious emphasis. The lessons look forwards as well as back. The ominous reference to death, which "cummis behind and nippis thame be the nek" (2223) recalls earlier allusions and looks forward to others, especially the kite of "The Paddock and the Mouse." The last question, "Quhat is mair dirk than blind prosperitie?" (2228), increases the gloom and darkness of the Narrator's mood and the atmosphere of the

Fables, as it is added to the cluster of images of unexpected misfortune and the threat of death. It recalls the transformation of the mice's feast, as "the cadgear cummis behind" (2226) may remind us of the cat.

In the later fables we may wonder if the Narrator has much to offer which is new. Certainly his lessons are stated in fresh ways, with other emphases, but most of the morals differ only in details from those already given. Several threads run through the *moralitates* and may be discerned in various places, stressing first one and then another of the themes, in obvious or obscure messages and using a variable symbolism. The earliest fables carry all the Narrator's messages, but in covert form. In "The Cock and the Jasp," the Narrator urges his audience to search for hidden knowledge; in "The Two Mice," he unobtrusively states his themes of deception, misfortune in the midst of joy, and the virtue of contented and dutiful living. Deception in the second fable is unintentional self-delusion, later developed as deliberate and malicious deceit, a prominent theme of the fox fables, leading to the particular case of false friends. Sudden misfortune eventually becomes the threat of death, leading to the separation of the soul and body. The dutiful life is seen to include obligations to God and one's fellow man. The world is mentioned frequently: as a natural background for the activities of the characters and as an active and generally malign force in shaping them. The world and its fleshly temptations imply the presence of the devil in various guises. Since the symbolism is inconsistent, detailed exposition is often necessary.

The rural mouse is misled by deceptive appearances, but her experiences are unlike those of the cock who finds the jasp; she realizes and suffers for her error, unlike the unenlightened cock. The theme of deception is developed through examples which show increasing malevolence in the flattery of the fox, practised on Chantecleir and the wolf, elaborating the motif of false friends. In "The Fox, the Wolf, and the Cadger," the fox is seen not merely as a human flatterer but as the world, which deceives man, making him forget death; in "The Fox, the Wolf, and the Husbandman," he represents the devil. The comments on deception become more serious than the general disapproval which follows a light-hearted tale such as that of "The Cock and the Fox." Although we have no sympathy for its wolf victim, we do not find that the tale of "The Fox, the Wolf, and the Cadger" has a happy ending; its *moralitas* gives a severe jolt, with the suggestion of damage to man's soul rather than to his body, made through the deeds of the most obvious villains of the *Fables*, and showing that the brutal, stupid wolf is easily duped by the resourceful fox.

We find the strongest warning against false friends in the *moralitas* of "The Paddock and the Mouse," emphasized in the three stanzas which recall the *moralitas* of "The Two Mice." These stanzas are alike in the use of the

ballade form and in expressing their thoughts with vivid images which draw
on the experiences of everyday life, including "[t]hy awin fyre, freind, thocht
it be bot ane gleid" (389) and "better beir of stane the barrow" (2915). In
both *moralitates* the tone is intimate, with the audience addressed, in the
singular, as "freind" and "my brother," but the mood of the stanzas in
"The Two Mice" is comforting, quite unlike that of "The Paddock and the
Mouse," which expresses necessary fear and suspicion. The warning against
deceit is repeated tersely and shockingly in "Ane silkin toung, ane hart of
crueltie, / Smytis more sore than ony schot of arrow" (2922–2923), and
the difference in mood is emphasized by the lines which form a concluding
chorus to the stanzas. Those of "The Two Mice" refer to the happiness
which may come from contentment "with small possessioun," whereas those
of "The Paddock and the Mouse" warn against "ane wickit marrow." The
contrast parallels the increasing gravity of the *Fables* and the Narrator's
diminishing hope for earthly life. The country mouse is saved by good
fortune and her wits, and her adventure ends in contentment, after she has
learned a lesson; the mouse of the last fable is the victim of a toad and a
kite, an unnatural and a natural enemy, and her helplessness reflects the
Narrator's pessimism.

Contentment is seen from several angles in the *moralitates*. Although
the cock is condemned for satisfaction with his lot, the country mouse is
praised. Lowrence is shot while he is sleeping contentedly and complacently,
and in the *moralitas* of "The Fox and the Wolf" he is condemned, but for
the sin of abusing the sacrament of confession, not for taking the goatherd's
kid. The lion of "The Lion and the Mouse" is censured for the complacency
which leads to negligence and eventually to his being trapped. Similarly,
the birds of "The Preaching of the Swallow" are shown to be neglectful,
in the contentment and optimism which make them ignore the swallow's
warning and the malevolence of the churl. The wether, on the other hand,
is ridiculed for his outrageous idea of pretending to be a sheep dog, and brutally punished for trying to "clym sa hie." The mouse of "The Paddock and
the Mouse" is another creature wanting to improve her lot, and, although
it may seem that she shows commendable ambition in attempting to taste
sweeter food, her bizarre means of travelling to it can only bring calamity.
The Narrator's apparently contradictory views on contentment and ambition are resolved in his exposition of the allegory of her journey across the
stream. The soul, here the mouse, must aspire to a better life, but is always weighed down by the body, represented by the evil toad. The soul's
passage can only be accomplished when it is separated from the body by
death. But death too is seen ambiguously; here it is the kite, swooping on
the two helpless creatures, with no feeling but hunger, not speaking as they
have done, but merely uttering its natural cry "pew." This appearance of

death seems terrifyingly general, and comes unemotionally and inevitably to the good and evil characters of the tale. In spite of the suggestion, made so often, that happiness and a better life can only be achieved in heaven, only the perfectly prepared soul could welcome death: "The saull rycht fane wald be brocht ouer, I wis, / Out of this warld into the heuinnis blis" (2960–2961). The body must inevitably struggle against it.

Related to the theme of contentment is that of the possibility of misfortune in the midst of joy, the "fitchis myngit ... with nobill seid," so that sorrows may come with a capricious twist of Fortune's wheel. There are cautions against troubles which can be avoided, as in "The Preaching of the Swallow," and the strongest statement of Fortune's influence comes in the *moralitas* of "The Paddock and the Mouse."[5] But man is not shown only as the victim of his own helplessness, he is also subjected to many temptations, which are to be resisted, generally classified as those of the world, and including most distractions from spiritual duties. The world is expressed in a variety of symbols and shown to be both attractive and threatening—God's gift or empty delusion. In "The Trial of the Fox," the world is the "wyld lyoun," an ambiguous figure, giving justice with great temporal power but shunned by the mare, who represents "men of contemplatioun," and a cause of driving ambition among earthly rulers who strive

> Sum for to reull, and sum to raxe and ring,
> Sum gadderis geir, sum gold, sum vther gude;
> To wyn this warld, sum wirkis as thay wer wod.   (1108–1110)

There is less ambiguity in "The Lion and the Mouse," where

> The fair forest with leuis, lowne and le,
> With foulis sang and flouris ferlie sweit,
> Is bot the warld and his prosperitie,
> As fals plesance, myngit with cair repleit.
> Richt as the rois with froist and wynter weit
> Faidis, swa dois the warld, and thame desauis
> Quhilk in thair lustis maist confidence hauis.   (1580–1586)

The beauty of the world is transitory, and the fading of the rose again suggests the coming of sorrow after joy. The tale of "The Preaching of the Swallow," in its prologue, speaks of the world as God's creation, perfectly designed for the service of man. However, in *moralitas* of "The Fox, the Wolf, and the Cadger," the fable which follows it, "the warld ... stewart to the man, / Quhilk makis man to haif na mynd of deid" (2210–2211), is the

---

[5] See Ch. IX: 95

evil fox, using the temptation of the non-existent herring, "the gold sa reid" (2213), to distract gullible man. In the next fable, the symbols and their messages are more sinister and intense. Instead of the fair forest we find "The wodds waist, quhairin wes the wolf wyld, / Ar wickit riches, quhilk all men gaipis to get" (2441–2441), and the illusion of the great cheese is covetousness, which deludes man, just as the wolf was tricked. The world in "The Paddock and the Mouse" is the water, which is almost powerful enough to overwhelm man's soul, yet does not eventually bring death to separate it from the body.

The Narrator's strongest and most specific preaching is found in the *moralitates* of the fables concerning sheep. That of "The Sheep and the Dog" makes detailed comment on the corruption of the courts with which Henryson was familiar, and that of "The Wolf and the Wether" ridicules the presumptuous seekers of advancement, warning that each man must know himself and his place in the social structure, essentially a narrower restatement of the message of "The Two Mice." "The Wolf and the Lamb," with an opposite perspective, concerns the obligations of those whose position is powerful, giving instruction and admonition to wolves of three kinds who oppress the weak. This *moralitas* is the longest, and most specifically recounts the sufferings of the victims, telling of the abuse of law and the plight of poor tenants through a sequence of particular details:

His hors, his meir, he man len to the laird,
To drug and draw in cairt and cariage;
His seruand or his self may not be spaird
To swing and sweit withoutin meit or wage:
Thus how he standis in labour and bondage
That scantlie may he purches by his maill
To leue vpon dry breid and watter caill.   (2749–2755)

There is none of the optimism of the *moralitas* of "The Lion and the Mouse"; the poor seem entirely defeated by their ill-treatment, and there is no sign that they could threaten anyone in power. There is a resemblance, though, in the closing prayer:

God, as thov all rychteous prayer heiris,
Mot saif our king, and gif him hart and hand
All sic wolfis to banes of the land.   (2774–2776)

The lessons described above are the strands which run through the *moralitas*. They are all connected, and we may wonder how many times they must be repeated to erring man. In the first *moralitas* the Narrator tells his audience to seek wisdom, the gift needed to enable them to perceive the lessons around them. He must, however, be more specific; in the *moralitas* of "The Two Mice" he states or hints at the themes he considers most important, although the prominence of the virtue of contentment overshadows other teachings, making it seem that the fable has only one moral. The strands of reasoning are drawn out and elaborated through the series of *moralitates* and eventually brought together in that of "The Paddock and the Mouse," which addresses the topics of deception, contentment, duty, temptation, the world and death, the inevitable separation of soul and body, for which all must prepare. If man were perfect, then the first fable alone would suffice. Clearly this is not so; humanity's imperfections must be shown: in an apparently simple way in "The Two Mice," and with increasing clarity and specificity until the strands come together in "The Paddock and the Mouse," a grim coincidence in this fable of the tying and breaking of the thread of life.

We may see then that varied repetition is a part of the Narrator's method. He looks at the vices with which he deals from several angles, because man is tempted away from perfection in a number of ways; for example, in speaking of deception, he speaks of known deceivers, false friends, the world, and man's deluded self. The variety and elaboration of the tales, building on Aesop's bare framework, give an idea of the complications and difficulties of life.

If we wonder why the teachings of the first two *moralitates* are later elaborated, we need only look again at the title of the work. Henryson composed a collection of *moral* fables. He could simply have stated the moral lessons which he thought deserved attention, but this would only give another sermon. There were sermons already and still sinners. He even refrained from making the *moralitates* excessively complicated, suggesting, in "The Paddock and the Mouse," that any morals remaining may be left to the friars. The tales are the longer part of the work, with the important functions of attracting and holding the attention of the audience. The *moralitates* give bare moral statements, and they are essential certainly; but the *tales* create the characters which show man in his most obnoxious, ridiculous, pathetic and endearing aspects, adding great force to the symbolism and teaching. We could not take away either the tales or their morals without doing grave damage to the fable cycle. Without the tales, there would be only stern moralizing, unlikely to attract the attention of an audience in need of it. Without the morals, we should have only a collection of animal stories, engaging but superficial and apparently unrelated.

Thus the poet needs the complete work to achieve his effect. The Narrator must engage the audience with the tales, and show, in the *moralitates*, the lessons and ways of exploring other such stories and the circumstances of their lives. His methods are often those of the schoolroom, although he surely speaks to adults, not children. We may agree with Kinsley's comment, "It is easy enough to see the moralizing dominie in Henryson's work; but the hard ironist is also there" (Kinsley, 1955: 21). The Narrator of the *Moral Fables* frequently acts as a moralizing dominie, and irony works to sharpen and enliven his teaching, as he strives to makes his audience more perceptive and more dutiful, guiding them to follow his thoughts and apply his methods until he dismisses his pupils, saying to each one, "Adew, my freind."

barely at apt in adults, not children. Yet ... may agree with Finsley's comments. It is ... enough to see the moralising comments in Hutcheson's work; but the final point is also stated (Finsley, 1868, p.5). The ... of the Moral Fatter ... as a moralising describer, and in my works he shares in instructing his teaching, as he strives to make his audience more perceptive and more dutiful guiding them to look ... his thoughts and apply his methods until he dismisses his pupils, saying to each one of them, my friend ...

VI
The wolf's progress

The characters of the *Moral Fables* are taken from Aesop's *Fables* and from the stories of Reynard the fox, found originally in the *Roman de Renart*. Henryson translates them to his world of fifteenth-century Scotland, retaining many of their characteristics and adding others which fit his time and place and the lessons he wishes to derive from the tales. We find he retains such accustomed symbolic associations as the lamb as a figure for suffering humanity and the cock for a proud and foolish man, but that some symbols are idiosyncratic and unexpected. The symbolic function of characters may grow, with later expositions assuming and developing those which have previously been stated. In discussing Henryson's use of symbols, I wish to concentrate on the wolf, who appears more often than any other character, as a victim of the fox and a predator of the sheep, and whose character shows an alarming development.

Among the beasts of the *Fables*, the wolf is the one which could most credibly provoke fear in the Narrator's original audience. There was good reason to dread the natural creature, not only as a predator to farm animals, but also as a beast which might attack man. Although the lion is more powerful, he is too exotic to provoke genuine fear, and any awe he arouses is more likely to be that due to the sovereign he represents. The natural fox was a threat to smaller creatures and was considered vermin, but he could not be thought dangerous to man. The "grit violence" which Lowrence does to the widow of "The Cock and the Fox" is "in pyking of pultrie baith day and nicht" (423). The legends of wolves stress their strength and ferocity, with the most gruesome being those of werewolves, terrifying because the creature is man transformed, and able to assume either form. We can assume the acquaintance of author and audience with this alarming creature, because the werewolf is among the first to bow before the lion, with others having the characteristics of men and beasts:

> The minotaur, ane monster meruelous,
> Bellerophont, that beist of bastardrie,
> The warwolff, and the pegase perillous[1]   (887–889)

---

[1] I.W.A. Jamieson comments that these creatures, showing characteristics of men and beasts, give striking examples of "the evil mortal changed (transformit) into an animal: the man in whose mind sin is so fixed that he 'in brutal beist be transformit' (*Prolog* 56)" (Jamieson, 1964: 229).

The wolf appears in both sources and so is in the fables of Aesopic and Reynardian origin. Aesop shows him as a vicious wrongdoer, and he inspires fear in the weaker creatures who are his victims. In the *Roman de Renart* he is Isengrim, a brutal villain, but also a victim of the wiles of the fox, his nephew, in spite of superior strength. He is the butt of Renart's schemes, easily duped and often injured. This wolf, too, is a rogue, but a stupid, brutal one, with none of the flair shown by the fox. Henryson shows that the fox, in his dealings with the wolf, personifies bad influences on man's nature. He represents "temptationis" (1132) in "The Trial of the Fox," "the warld ... [q]uhilk makis man to haif na mynd of deid" (2210–2211) in "The Fox, the Wolf, and the Cadger," and finally "the Feind" (2431) in "The Fox, the Wolf, and the Husbandman"; all these are influences which can evade the law and overcome frail humanity's attempts to resist them.

The wolf is a powerful and eventually very specific symbol for the worst in man; and we may follow his progress, seeing how man's baser aspects are manipulated to become dominant. This is seen through his encounters with adversaries of two kinds, with superior intellect but inferior physical strength—the foxes, who can always outwit him, and three sheep characters with courage and varying intelligence, but insufficient guile. The nature of the wolf changes in the fables where he is deceived and manipulated by the fox, and characteristics are retained in those which follow and involve the sheep characters—"The Sheep and the Dog," "The Wolf and the Wether" and "The Wolf and the Lamb," where the wolf is neither encouraged nor restrained by external influences.[2] As the sequence continues, the fox's manipulation becomes more outrageous and the wolf's dealings with the sheep more cruel, less justified, and also more specific, symbolizing the actions of particular wrongdoers. The wolf's story and the growth of an increasingly specific symbolism are two of the continuing threads which run through the work. He is used as a figure for corrupt and foolish clergy, debased court officials, man as a dupe, easily deceived by appeals to his vanity and greed, and, at his worst, he represents man with power which he can use to oppress the weak. His presence, with the progressive assumption of characteristics previously revealed, is another theme which lends support to the acceptance of the Bassandyne order of the *Fables*.

---

[2] In general, the wolf is influenced by the fox in fables of Reynardian origin, and these are followed by Aesopic fables where he acts independently. H.H. Roerecke classifies "The Cock and the Fox," "The Fox and the Wolf," "The Trial of the Fox," "The Fox, the Wolf, and the Cadger," "The Fox, the Wolf, and the Husbandman" and "The Wolf and the Wether" as Reynardian (Roerecke, 1969: 137–141). Such a designation gives a more balanced grouping of Aesopic and Reynardian fables in the first and second halves of the fable collection. Denton Fox disagrees with this classification of "The Cock and the Fox" and "The Wolf and the Wether" (Fox, 1981: lxxx). I shall refer to the fables involving Lowrence and the wolf simply as fox and wolf fables.

The most significant influence on the wolf, Lowrence the fox, is introduced in "The Cock and the Fox," and the fable displays his greatest asset,
his agile intellect. Although he is eventually outfoxed by the vain and susceptible Chantecleir, he escapes to carry on his scandalous career, which
the audience perceives as a satisfactory conclusion in all respects. We are
well prepared for his second appearance in "The Fox and the Wolf," the
fable also known as "The Confession of the Fox." We know that Lowrence
has no respect for lawful bounds or authority, can juggle with the truth,
and is a self-reliant rascal who can improvise a way out of most difficulties.
Thus it is somewhat surprising to find him in a brief moment of depression,
after casting his horoscope, saluting a wandering wolf as "Freir Volff Waitskaith," to request the sacrament of confession. We must always suspect
that the fox offers exaggerated courtesy for his own ends to one he considers
his intellectual inferior, and the unrepentant confession and the bargain he
strikes over his penance confirm these suspicions.

The wolf was already a popular figure for anti-clerical satire, when Henryson wrote of him.[3] His colouring, strength and sinister reputation all lent
themselves to this use as a symbol for spiritual power abused, a use which
may begin with the biblical metaphor of the false prophets who are wolves
in sheep's clothing (Matt. 7: 15), and continues at least as far as Milton's
reference to "the grim wolf with privy paw" ("Lycidas," line 128). The
inflated compliments with which Freir Volff Waitskaith is greeted,

> '3e ar the lanterne and the sicker way
> Suld gyde sic sempill folk as me to grace;
> 3our bair feit and 3our russet coull off gray,
> 3our lene cheik, 3our paill and pietious face,
> Schawis to me 3our perfite halines;
> For weill wer him that anis in his lyue
> Had hap to 3ow his sinnis for to schryue,'   (677–682)

are hardly more than gentle teasing when we compare them with the savage
attacks he must endure in later fables. The picture given here is only of
a foolishly flexible confessor, easily managed by the unrepentant candidate
for absolution, but we must not ignore the effects on a medieval audience
of references to clerical wolves in other works, which could make him both
more ludicrous and more threatening. We accept the wolf as a scoundrel

---

[3] Several examples are mentioned by John Block Friedman (Friedman, 1967: 552).
K. Varty describes the wolf's appearances in clerical disguise in Rutebeuf's *Renard le
Bestourné*, "a brief and bitter attack on the mendicant orders" (Varty, 1967: 22), and
in the incident where Reynard and Isengrim play priests and Isengrim rings the church
bells (Varty, 1967: 58). He also mentions that Isengrim carries the cross at Reynard's
funeral (Varty, 1967: 85).

and no match for Lowrence, but although he is ridiculous, we do not find him appealing or likeable in any way. Perhaps this too is influenced by impressions from outside the work, from other literary references and from the knowledge that a natural wolf, if confronted, could be a threat to man, whereas a fox would prefer to escape with his prey.

The pliable wolf is an ideal companion for the fox, and they are seen next in "The Trial of the Fox," the fable which follows. This fox is not, in fact, the one who appeared in "The Fox and the Wolf," since he was shot by the goatherd, and the Narrator primly introduces the protagonist of this tale as

> ane sone, the quhilk in lemanrye
> He [Lowrence] gottin had in purches priuelie,
> And till his name wes callit Father-war,
> That luifit weill with pultrie to tig and tar.   (799–802)

As the tale proceeds, we see that Father-war assumes, along with his father's hunting territory, Lowrence's name and other characteristics, so that he is indistinguishable from any fox appearing in any place in the *Fables*. We may regard them all as aspects of the vulpine intellect and character, each answering to the name "Tod Lowrie," with the same intentions and abilities, exerting an effect which persists in spite of all efforts made against it. Similarly, we may consider the wolf as a developing and composite character, presenting a range of human evils.

"The Trial of the Fox" displays the wolf's vanity, which is used to ensure that he receives the mare's kick, the first of the injuries to which the fox entices him. He is easily led and we feel no regret, sharing the laughter of the court at his misfortune. The bleeding scalp of "this new-maid doctour off diuinitie" (1052) gives the opportunity for more jokes at the expense of the clergy, as the lion draws the morals, "The greitest clerkis ar not the wysest men; / The hurt off ane happie the vther makis" (1064–1065). Although the wolf hears the fox's confession before his execution, he seems in no sense superior to Lowrence, an impression reinforced when the Narrator identifies him in the *moralitas* as sensuality.

In "The Sheep and the Dog," the Aesopic fable which follows, the wolf and fox retain their Reynardian natures, and the wolf's symbolic function is extended. The fox makes only a brief appearance as "clerk and noter in the cause" (1174), but the Narrator describes him in the *moralitas* as "this fals tod, of quhilk I spak befoir" (1279). The wolf again depicts abused authority, this time as judge in a corrupt court which suggests ecclesiastical and temporal jurisdiction. Although the dog is the helpless sheep's direct antagonist, the wolf, as judge, exerts greater power. He presides over a court where the officers are sinister figures: predators such as "Schir Corbie Rauin

... maid apparitour" (1160) and other birds of prey, the kite and vulture; all the creatures are ludicrously unfitted for their tasks, such as the bear, used elsewhere as a figure for sloth, but here sent to consult court records.[4] Although the judge proclaims himself "partles off fraud and gyle" (1155), he is malevolent and overbearing and clearly not disposed to give justice. The sheep's case, although clearly and boldly stated, has no chance of success, and the wolf represents man corrupted by power and evil company misusing his authority.

In the fox and wolf fables we see that the effects of the fox's influence are harmful to the wolf, beginning with ridicule and the mare's kick and leading to beating and stranding in the well; but in the sheep fables which follow them the wolf is free to do harm and the sheep are his victims, with the scale of his predations steadily increasing. In his encounters with sheep the worst and best aspects of humanity are illustrated, most sharply in "The Wolf and the Lamb," where the victim is the most helpless and innocent of the sheep characters.

The second pair of fox and wolf fables, "The Fox, the Wolf, and the Cadger" and "The Fox, the Wolf, and the Husbandman," shows the fox's corrupting influence most clearly, and this effect is imitated in the patterns of speech between the two characters which recall earlier references and are suggested again in later tales.[5] The pattern is set in the opening dialogue of "The Fox, the Wolf, and the Cadger," when the "reuand volff" (1953) greets the fox, anxious to appoint Lowrence as his steward. The wolf always tries to assert mastery, stressing his power by the use of the familiar "thow" form of address. His speeches have a harsh quality, with introductions such as " 'Na,' quod the volff," using discordant sounds which suggest the snarling of the natural wild beast. In spite of his assumed authority he must continually shift his ground, using a jumble of proverbs and arguments to compel the fox to serve him. In contrast, the fox slides smoothly and confidently into his speeches, introduced by the alliterative " 'Schir,' said the foxe." We notice later that "quod" is used of the fox in his rare undeceptive moments, such as his farewell to the cadger, " 'Now,' quod the foxe, 'I schreu me and we meit!'" (2091). "Said" often introduces speeches of persuasion, for instance those of the husbandman; more significantly, it is linked with the words of the wolf, when his thoughts begin to follow those of the fox.

The repeated patterns add to the effect of a game for two players, which we see whenever the two characters are together. The exchanges are unequal contests in which the only challenge to the fox is to find new

---

[4] This is observed by E.N. Daugherty, who also notes the ferocity of both the bear and the badger (Daugherty, 1977: 70–71).

[5] Marilyn Mumford comments on the comic effects of these syntactical patterns (Blanchot/Graf, 1978: 246–248).

and more bizarre ways to demonstrate his intellectual superiority. In "The Fox, the Wolf, and the Cadger," he allows the wolf the illusion of dominance, always addresses his would-be master in the polite "зow" style, and accepts the office of steward after the wolf's angry rejection of his spurious excuses. He even agrees to swear loyalty to the wolf, with the ambiguous words:

> 'Зit sall I sweir, suppois it be nocht neid,
> Be Iuppiter, and on pane off my heid,
> I sall be treu to зou quhill I be deid.'   (2025–2027)

The fox's speeches grow longer than the wolf's and are consistently confident, plausible and apparently respectful, in the style Lowrence has perfected for his intellectual inferiors. He soon induces the wolf to follow him for the menial task of gathering herrings thrown from the cadger's cart and later for the ridiculous pretence of death.

The exchanges between the two rogues form an enjoyably repetitive pattern which offers great scope to a speaking narrator. This tale particularly recommends itself as one to be heard, suggesting the interaction of a melodramatic performer and a receptive audience. The story is told largely through the speeches of the characters, for whom one can imagine a range of tones of voice, expressing such feelings as the smooth assurance of the fox, the exploited greed of the wolf and the rage of the cadger. The Narrator's direct comments in the tale are only those on the wolf's greed, "He that of ressoun can not be content, / Bot couetis all, is abill all to tyne" (2189–2190), and the fox's success, "I le, or ellis he wes efterward fyne" (2193). Descriptive passages are generally scanty, but an important exception is that of the pretence of death, employed by the fox (2049–2055) and later by the wolf (2158–2167), after Lowrence's instructions (2133–2144). We may imagine the Narrator's lingering on the wary glance around, the choice of a conspicuous place to lie on the road, the perfect stillness and the lolling tongue. Similarly, we may imagine the audience's anticipation of each detail, especially in the last description, that of the inveigled wolf, to be delivered, no doubt, with extravagant expression:

> With that the volff gird vp sone and to gay,
> And caist ane cumpas about the cadgear far;
> Syne raucht him in the gait, or he come nar.

> He laid his halfheid sicker hard and sad,
> Syne straucht his four feit fra him, and his heid,
> And hang his toung furth as the foxe him bad;
> Als styll he lay as he wer verray deid,
> Rakkand na thing off the carlis fauour nor feid,

Bot euer vpon the nekhering he thinkis,
And quyte forȝettis the foxe and all his wrinkis.   (2158–2167)

The reader easily succumbs to the illusion of being one of a listening audience, enjoying the performance of the speaking Narrator, an illusion to
which I shall return later. These retellings, like the exchanges of the fox
and the wolf, give something of the nature of a well-loved children's story,
where "repetition, the re-experiencing of something identical, is clearly in
itself a source of pleasure."[6] The abrupt conclusion to smooth talking and
amusing description is the brutal beating of the wolf, followed by the laughter of the fox. The Narrator reveals in the *moralitas* that the wolf is "ane
man, but leis" (2206), but the fox is the world, and we see how easily man
is won by the world when it appeals to his greed.

    In the next fable, "The Fox, the Wolf, and the Husbandman," the wolf
is subjected to further temptations and ridicule. It is not difficult for the
fox to persuade him to claim the oxen cursed by the husbandman and
later distract him with the promise of an illusory cheese. The established
pattern may still be discerned, and Lowrence needs only one sentence to
accomplish his first trick, "To tak ȝone bud ... it wer na skaith" (2249).
The wolf's greed for such preposterous prey is enough, and he is eager to
challenge the unfortunate husbandman. As usual, the wolf's manner is
overbearing, emphasized by his addressing the husbandman as "thow." He
backs his claim with a recitation of proverbs, and has no understanding of
his false position. We are reminded of previous fables by such characteristic
openings as " 'Carll,' quod the volff" (2280) and " 'Weill,' quod the volff"
(2306), balanced again by " 'Schir,' said the tod" (2301). The fox's cajolery
is at its most brilliant in this tale, as he persuades his two dupes to accept
him as a judge, the husbandman to bribe him for a favourable judgement,
and the wolf to be satisfied with the prospect of a huge cheese. This last
operation is the most difficult and is eventually accomplished in an exchange
which economically and elegantly illustrates his control of the patterns of
speech. We see that Lowrence appears to follow the wolf, but that at last
the wolf's thoughts and speech are led, with the fox having the last word:

'Weill,' quod the volff, 'it is aganis my will
That ȝone carll for ane cabok suld ga quyte.'
'Schir,' quod the tod, 'ȝe tak it in nane euill,
For, be my saull, ȝour self had all the wyte.'
Than said the volff, 'I bid na mair to flyte,
Bot I wald se ȝone cabok off sic pryis.'
'Schir,' said the tod, 'he tauld me quhair it lyis.'   (2364–2370)

---

[6] The view of Sigmund Freud (Strachey, 1955: 36).

At the well, their last exchanges recall the previous pattern, with the fox's speeches introduced by "'Schir,' said the tod" (2385) and "'Schir,' said Lowrence" (2393), while the wolf snarls greedily ("'Na,' quod the volff," 2399) and orders the fox into the well. Lowrence's last trick is a variation of the nekhering ruse, but in this tale he does not merely laugh in secret. There is no further need for pretence or persuasion when his victim is stranded at the bottom of the well. The tod can take his leave in impudent style, reported with the "quod" which has been associated with the one who considers himself in charge: "'Schir,' quod the foxe, 'thus fairis it off fortoun: / As ane cummis vp, scho quheillis ane vther doun'" (2418–2419). The fox, identified now as "the Feind" (2431), does not appear again in the *Fables*, but the wolf is seen twice.

In the *moralitas* of "The Fox, the Wolf, and the Husbandman" the wolf is revealed as

> ane wickit man
> Quhuilk dois the pure oppres in euerie place,
> And pykis at thame all querrellis that he can,
> Be rigour, reif, and vther wickitnes.   (2427–2430)

These characteristics are developed in the sheep fables which follow, shown with some grim comedy in "The Wolf and the Wether" and tragically in "The Wolf and the Lamb." In his encounters with weaker sheep characters, the wolf is a symbol of wrongdoing which is both vicious and successful. When he attempts to bully the fox, we know that he will fail, but no lasting harm can come to a wolf whose adversary is a sheep.

In "The Wolf and the Wether" he is temporarily deceived by one who is weaker, but the wether himself is deceived by his early success, and so does not understand his false and dangerous position. The foolish wether's use of trickery resembles Chantecleir's and Lowrence's but, unlike them, he does not know when to retreat. The Narrator introduces a wether with good intentions and a very hungry wolf. Both creatures have some mitigating circumstances to explain their actions at the beginning of the tale, but all excuses are swept away as the tale and *moralitas* proceed. In spite of his praiseworthy motive, the wether fails as a dog and a sheep, since a true sheepdog would return to his flock with the lamb and a true sheep would stay with his fellows. The deluded wether's unfounded and unbounded pride makes him challenge the wolf in a speech which resembles the wolf's:

> 'Na,' quod the wedder, 'in faith we part not swa:
> It is not the lamb, bot the, that I desyre;
> I sall cum neir, for now I se the tyre.'   (2534–2536)

The reckless creature seems almost to be snarling, and rashly uses the familiar form of address to his natural enemy. We may note as a verbal

sign of the wolf's fear that he addresses the wether as "ȝow" until his last
speech, before he viciously breaks the wether's neck. The helpless sheep can
offer only a humble and ineffectual excuse to his enraged adversary when
the dog's skin is lost:

> 'For quhat enchessoun this doggis skyn haue ȝe borne?'
> 'Maister,' quod he, 'bot to haue playit with ȝow;
> I ȝow requyre that ȝe nane vther trow.'   (2557–2559)

This excuse is of no more use to the wether than it was to Lowrence in
"The Trial of the Fox" (1079). The end is inevitable, yet the death of the
wether seems only an act of malicious revenge, since the Narrator does not
tell us that he is eaten, although the wolf was described as desperately
hungry (2511, 2514 and 2526). There is little in the tale to recommend the
wolf, although we may feel some sympathy for the foolhardy wether and
be surprised, at first, by the Narrator's harsh condemnation of his reckless
bravado. We should look carefully at the *moralitas* to see how the lesson
is delivered. While it warns against the delusions of pretentious upstarts,
the advice also reminds the audience of the changes which may come even
to the lives of powerful men:

> Bot ȝit nane wait how lang that reull will ring;
> Bot he was wyse that bad his sone considder:
> Bewar in welth, for hall benkis ar rycht slidder.   (2606–2608)

This warning suggests a general admonition, intended for every member of
society, including those powerful ones represented by the wolf, to attend to
the duties of his rank within the feudal system.

The wolf's last appearance shows him entirely as a tyrant, using his
power unjustly against the lamb, who is intelligent, brave and right, but
physically too weak to stand against him. The wolf always wants to take
the lamb at the stream and eventually dispenses with the formality of an
excuse. The two creatures are contrasted in biased introductory passages
and in the wolf's threats and accusations, countered with the reasoned
replies of the lamb.[7] This tale too is advanced largely through the speeches
of its protagonists, but their dialogue shows none of the comic effects of the
fox's persuasion. The lamb's mild and cogent answers serve only to enrage
the wolf, whose replies suggest the growling of a wild beast.

In the wolf's last recorded actions we may recall his first—the amusing
sacramental satire of the fox's confession. Now there is a gruesome parody
of the eucharist, and the wolf leaves in peace, having shown his power. The
shocking nature of this scene is offset a little by the nearest approach to

---

[7] See Ch. III: 20–21.

humour in this fable, the hint of a pun, which may remind us of the joyful mice who, "quhen thay disposit wer to dyne, / Withoutin grace, thay wesche and went to meit" (267–268). The lamb's death is tragic, but saved from sentimentality by the brevity and slight ambiguity of the description:

> The selie lamb culd do na thing bot bleit:
> Sone wes he hedit; the volff wald do na grace;
> Syne drank his blude and off his flesche can eit
> Quhill he wes full; syne went his way on pace.
> Off his murther quhat sall we say, allace?   (2700–2704)

Any addition to this account would be superfluous. The lamb is already well known as a victim, in general and particularly Christian symbolism, and the reference to the consumption of his blood and flesh implies blasphemy as well as murder. His allegorical function as a representative of the oppressed poor is fully expounded in the *moralitas*, which has the sternest condemnation of the wolf. The Narrator speaks of wolves, "fals extortioneris" (2711), of three kinds: "fals peruerteris of the lawis" (2715), "mychtie men, haifand aneuch plentie" (2729) and "men of heritage" (2742); and this is the most specific of the *moralitates*, being directed to individual wrongdoers rather than to the audience in general.

Throughout the *Fables* we never find a reason to approve of the wolf. We have no sympathy for his misfortunes; and his susceptibility to the fox's blandishments makes a poor excuse for his misdeeds. In fact we are pleased when his actions harm himself, and despise him when he uses his power against the weaker sheep characters. We could choose to regard these actions as caused by persisting evil influence on his character, but there are no suggestions of mitigation beyond hunger and the terror induced by the wether. The wolf represents all the traits we despise in ourselves, given full scope by the acquisition of authority. The growth in his capacity to do harm is alarming, from his first appearance as an amusingly rascally friar to his final identification as a powerful oppressor of the poor, and it illustrates the Narrator's most pessimistic view of humanity.

There are some warnings to wolves in the allusions to the unpredictable turning of Fortune's wheel in "The Wolf and the Wether" and also in the *moralitas* of "The Wolf and the Lamb":

> O thow grit lord, that riches hes and rent,
> Be nocht ane wolf, thus to deuoir the pure!
> Think that na thing cruell nor violent
> May in this warld perpetuallie indure.   (2763–2766)

These are brave words, but, like the lamb, the Narrator has greatest trust in an appeal to higher justice:

God keip the lamb, quhilk is the innocent,
From wolfis byit and men extortioneris;
God grant that wrangous men of fals intent
Be manifest, and punischit as effeiris;
And God, as thow all rychteous prayer heiris,
Mot saif our king, and gif him hart and hand
All sic wolfis to banes of the land.   (2770–2776)

When he is influenced by the world, the temptations of the flesh and the devil, the wolf represents man at his weakest, spiritually; when he has authority, he is man at his strongest, temporally. He is always man at his worst, a convincingly universal symbol for the evil tendencies in every man, with characteristics which persist when identifiable influences have gone. He serves as a salutary and threatening warning. The Narrator exposes one of man's persisting dilemmas by showing us our capacity to despise the wolf while we admire both the power he gains and the skills of the personification of bad influences—the fox.

VII
The Narrator's world

As he creates and sustains the illusions of the worlds of the characters and the audience, the site of the Narrator's activities varies, and he may seem to speak from either of these worlds. He is at first more closely allied with the characters, but moves to join the audience as the sequence of the Bassandyne order proceeds, detaching himself from the frankly fictitious realm of the lion to associate himself with the audience and the truths he teaches in their domair. We find a number of places where his perspective changes, marked by a deliberate movement from one setting to the other, as the Narrator comes to be a part of the audience and sometimes even gives his task to another, when Aesop, the sheep and the swallow act as substitutes, and the lessons touch extremes of optimism and despair.

The movement of the Narrator towards his audience encourages and preserves the illusion of his own reality, as he leaves the patently imaginary speaking beasts he knows variously as witness, friend, host and even pupil. When he introduces himself in "The Prologue," the Narrator's deference to his "maisteris" suggests that he is not at one with the audience, and the telling of the first tales confirms that he is associated rather with their fanciful settings and characters. It is an ambiguous position, since he is not a character of the *Fables* as are the animals, not even as are the few human characters such as the widow, the fowler and the shepherd. He appears at times to be an eyewitness to the events and to know the participants. We notice this particularly in "The Two Mice," the second fable in the Bassandyne order.

Although he opens the tale with the formula, "Esope, myn authour, makis mentioun" (162), he speaks as one with closer contact than that of merely reading about the characters. His description of the rural mouse's dwelling is introduced with the words "I hard say" (197), as is the news of her return to it (358). The exclamation, "The hartlie cheir, Lord God! geue ȝe had sene / Beis kithit quhen thir sisteris twa war met" (190–191), suggests that he has seen this joyful meeting; and he appears to be part of the household in which the sisters feast when he mentions "Gib Hunter, our iolie cat" (326). The idea of personal experience of the events gives immediacy and the illusion of reality to a delightfully preposterous story; and the intimacy of address continues in the *moralitas*, given to "freindis," and speaking of homely joys which all would cherish. Although the town mouse is exposed as a snobbish upstart, she is ridiculed gently, and the moral stresses the positive value of contentment with a simple life, rather than such negative aspects of the tale as family divisions and abrupt reversals of fortune. The Narrator speaks as one who inhabits the setting of the tale; by investing it with so much contemporary detail, he prepares his audience, too, to find it familiar, and to recognize human counterparts of the characters.

Closer links with the characters are implied in allusions to events which take place out of sight, as in the Narrator's references to knowledge gained from the foxes. Lowrence has taught him astrology, as mentioned in "The Fox and the Wolf," in the account of the stars which give the ominous horoscope, "Thay wer ilk ane, as Lowrence leirnit me" (634). That fox's son, at first called "Father-war" (801), soon assumes the name and nature of his father; and the description of the beasts in his story, "The Trial of the Fox," is said to be "to me as Lowrence leird" (884). It is one of the enjoyable ironies of the *Fables* that the one who teaches their lessons has been instructed by their chief villain.

The site of Narrator's activity is seen to change in the central fables, where he temporarily gives up his function to others, and deliberately dissociates himself from the world of the tales to join his audience. These fables are "The Sheep and the Dog," "The Lion and the Mouse" and "The Preaching of the Swallow," and they differ from the other fables in their arrangement of tale and *moralitas*.

In this respect, "The Sheep and the Dog" is most like the others, since it varies only in the conclusion to its *moralitas*, where the Narrator speaks of seeing the shorn sheep and hearing his mournful, accusing prayers. The Narrator is a witness to this event, as to others previously mentioned, but the sheep's long speech, with its general conclusions about the plight of the poor, suggests that he has assumed the Narrator's role. The creature's only recourse is to pray for the oppressed poor, and this is the first *moralitas* to imply that there is no other hope. Previous *moralitates* have been more sanguine, generally anticipating earthly benefits for those who heed their teachings. The pessimistic conclusion may be given to the suffering sheep, rather than to the Narrator, to emphasize the change of mood and distinguish it from the earlier implications of a more just and hopeful life. As this fable ends, the Narrator is still in the world of the tale, but as an observer, not as a participant.

The next fable, "The Lion and the Mouse," begins with a prologue, and the Narrator takes care to place himself within its beautifully described setting. The audience must always be aware that *he* is the one who experiences the details of his surroundings. He sees the colours of the flowers; he hears the singing of the birds; he has the dream in which Aesop appears.

Repetition of personal pronouns makes the Narrator prominent, as in the stanza which describes his dreaming:

Me to conserue than fra the sonis heit,
Vnder the schaddow off ane hawthorne grene
I lenit doun amang the flouris sweit,
Syne maid a cors and closit baith my ene.
On sleip I fell amang thir bewis bene,
And in my dreme, me thocht come throw the schaw
The fairest man that euer befoir I saw.   (1342–1348)

The audience must rely completely on the Narrator for this tale, which comes not from Aesop's book but from his own lips, and is revealed in the dream which is being retold. Thus the relationship of dependence is emphasized and fostered, and the unusual introduction gives notice of an unusual fable to follow. It differs from others in showing gloom about man's shortcomings *before* the telling of the tale, when Aesop must be entreated to tell "ane prettie fabill / Concludand with ane gude moralitie" (1386–1387). He agrees, but only after referring to man's incorrigibility, in the question, "For quhat is it worth to tell ane fenʒeit taill, / Quhen haly preiching may na thing auaill?" (1389–1390). The tale Aesop tells is the prettiest and most hopeful of the collection, with prompt rewards on earth for the good deeds of both protagonists.

Although the Narrator is so prominent in the prologue to "The Lion and the Mouse," he takes no part in the telling of the tale, which is left entirely to Aesop. The moral interpretation, rebuking kings and commoners, is also Aesop's, and this is emphasized by the Narrator's question after the telling of the tale: "Maister, is thair ane moralitie / In this fabill?" (1570–1571). Thus he dissociates himself from tale and *moralitas*, yet makes himself essential in their delivery. Although there may have been an intention to put politically dangerous remarks into the mouth of an ancient and impartial authority to avoid trouble for the poet, it is also a part of the process of separation.[1] The Narrator is still the audience's link with Aesop, but he is detaching himself from the world of the tales and their characters. He removes himself geographically from the scene in the last lines of the fable, "And with that word he vanist and I woke; / Syne throw the schaw my iourney hamewart tuke" (1620–1621). The journey "hamewart," a word repeated in "The Preaching of the Swallow," takes the Narrator back to the world of men. Although he is always present in the *Fables*, he belongs with mankind rather than in the fable world, which he sees now only as an observer, not as one who participates in the action. This is emphasized

---

[1] See Ch. V: 43.

by his leaving not only the dream world of Aesop and the tale but also the
setting in which he had the dream, and in the style of later comments as
an observer of events in "The Preaching of the Swallow."

"The Preaching of the Swallow" begins with the preaching of the Narrator; and, unlike other fables, it offers teaching in general terms before
moving to the particular case of the tale, which tells more of the activities
of people than of birds. This part of the fable, although it differs in sense,
is not set apart as a distinctly separate section, as are the prologue to "The
Lion and the Mouse" or the *moralitates* of the other fables. It is a part of
the tale, told by the Narrator with his own experiences. Before he gives
an eyewitness account of the story of the swallow and the other birds, he
sets the scene with a general account of man's place in creation, not men-
tioning Aesop, but referring to Aristotle as an authority, "In *Metaphisik*
Aristotell sayis / That mannis saull is lyke ane bakkis ee" (1636-1637). His
main authority is clearly scriptural, and the style of his description of the
created universe resembles that of the Psalms. A change in the Narrator's
allegiance, his disengagement with the fabulous, is seen in the manner used
in his preaching, where he includes himself with the audience to whom he
speaks:

> Thairfoir our saull with sensualitie
> So fetterit is in presoun corporall,
> We may not cleirlie vnderstand nor se
> God as he is, nor thingis celestiall;
> Our mirk and deidlie corps materiale
> Blindis the spirituall operatioun,
> Lyke as ane man wer bundin in presoun.   (1629-1635)

Such lines give the impression that he belongs in the world of people rather
than that of the fable characters.

"The Preaching of the Swallow" is set in the world of living, working,
waking men, placed by God at the centre of the universe, with creation
ordained to serve them. The Narrator is simply repeating conventional
opinion when he tells his audience

> All creature he maid for the behufe
> Off man, and to his supportatioun
> In to this eirth, baith vnder and abufe,
> In number, wecht, and dew proportioun;
> The difference off tyme, and ilk seasoun
> Concorddand till our opurtunitie
> As daylie be experience we may se.   (1671-1677)

He links himself with those who hear him, as before, by the use of "our" and "we." The confident statement of God's good purposes makes an optimistic beginning to one of the most tragic of fables, which eventually shows man in the worst light—literally as a cruel butcher and allegorically as a figure for Satan. The seasons are described in stanzas which tell of temperate summer and autumn, and the harvests of Italy and France; but the audience's attention is more closely focused on the violent coming of winter to the countryside of Scotland, by the metaphor of the stripping of the land. Flora, Phoebus, Ceres and Bacchus have blessed the earlier seasons with mild weather and abundance, but Aeolus rips away the cover of foliage and deprives the mourning birds of their shelter. The image of stripping, which recurs throughout the *Fables*, also serves to remind us of the Narrator's function of exposing the messages hidden below the surface of the tales, from which the covering of fiction must be removed. The coming of spring is described in terms which are still more specific, referring to birds which gather as the weather softens, and this change in the season introduces the Narrator's part in the story, as he describes his own action of walking out to look at his surroundings.

The Narrator tells his story as a hidden observer, and shows clearly that his first interest is in man's place in nature. He tells of man's use of his surroundings and remarks, describing the work of those who plough and sow, "It wes grit ioy to him that luifit corne / To se thame labour, baith at euin and morne" (1725–1726). Seeing the birds is an unexpected benefit of his excursion, and he expresses surprise at hearing their discussion. To a member of the audience, reasoning, talking beasts might well be strange, but they should not cause amazement to one who has lived among such creatures, learned from them and given them a home. The Narrator's transition from the world of fables is stressed again when he concludes his account of the birds' conversation: "I tuke my club, and hamewart couth I carie, / Swa ferliand as I had sene ane farie" (1774–1775).

He takes his next journey in June, when the flax is ripening, and hears the swallow warn that the churl is a fowler who will prey on the birds. This scene, too, concludes with the Narrator's return to his own home, removed from the world of speaking, reasoning birds, when he tells us "I tuke my staff, quhen this wes said and done, / And walkit hame, for it drew neir the none" (1823–1824). The deliberate actions of taking his staff and preparing to leave his hiding place parallel the contrast between that eerie spot and the dwellings of men who have no animal disguises. The account of the work of the fowler and his wife, who pick and treat the flax, then spin it into thread to make nets, appear to show merely another part of man's use of the created world, similar to his work in the fields. The Narrator suggests no sinister purpose as he tells more of man's ingenuity and industry, speaking as an observer from the world of men. This attitude begins to change when he describes the coming of winter and the sufferings of the birds, who must now seek shelter and food. The fowler becomes a terrifying figure, swearing great oaths to take the birds, setting his nets and luring the starving creatures with chaff. The brutality which which he kills them reveals his cruelty.

The tale ends with the departure of the swallow, a character who assumes some of the Narrator's teaching role, saying

> 'Lo ... thus it happinnis mony syis
> On thame that will not tak counsall nor reid
> Off prudent men or clerkis that ar wyis.
> This grit perrell I tauld thame mair than thryis;
> Now ar thay deid, and wo is me thairfoir!'   (1882–1886)

while the Narrator remains with his audience to deliver the *moralitas*. The first line of this *moralitas*, "Lo, worthie folk, Esope, that nobill clerk" (1888), which mentions Aesop's teaching, implies a variation on the usual policy of presenting Aesop's tales and the Narrator's own *moralitas*. Here, as in "The Lion and the Mouse," awkward speeches seem to be put into Aesop's mouth. As Aesop rebukes a king in "The Lion and the Mouse," so in "The Preaching of the Swallow" he appears to condemn the fowler, who is exposed as Satan. This play relieves the Narrator of the embarrassment of such a revelation when he has previously spoken of man's place at the centre of creation and identified the churl with man using God's gifts. The moral gives an exposition of the tale which describes the growth of sin, which resembles that of the seed, and shows the birds, who try to satisfy their hunger with chaff, to be wretched men pursuing empty pleasures, who will be "put in Luceferis bag, / And brocht to hell, and hangit be the crag" (1935–1936). The preaching swallow, by taking one of the offices of the Narrator, has allowed him to step further away from the fable world. The conclusion of the *moralitas* emphasizes both the Narrator's place in the world of men and the importance of the swallow, as they share the last message:

> Pray we thairfoir quhill we ar in this lyfe
> For four thingis: the first, fra sin remufe;
> The secund is to seis all weir and stryfe;
> The thrid is perfite cheritie and lufe;
> The feird thing is, and maist for our behufe,
> That is in blis with angellis to be fallow.
> And thus endis the preiching of the swallow.   (1944–1950)

The Narrator's prominence in the central fables has aroused some comment, including the remarks of Fox and Burrow (Fox, 1981: lxxviii; Burrow, 1975: 25). The variations in tone of "The Preaching of the Swallow" have led to an assumption of two narrators by Sandra Whipple Spanier:

> The "authoritative voice" ... speaks of earth from the remote regions of heaven and hell in the prologue and the *moralitas* respectively. The voice is impersonal, learned, philosophical, and theological—often speaking in abstractions and capable of transcending time and space. Most of the fable proper, which takes place on solid earth ... is narrated by a very human rustic wanderer, whose descriptions and perceptions are concrete and earthbound. (Spanier, 1979–80: 124)

The notion of these two narrators could perhaps be sustained, with difficulty, if this fable were the only one of the collection now in existence. In fact, the variations are among the moods, and hence the voices of the Narrator which are found throughout the *Fables*. The "authoritative voice" is heard in each *moralitas* and frequently in the tales, whenever the Narrator is acting as a teacher. We may think, for example, of the introductory stanzas of "The Cock and the Fox" which, like the third stanza of "The Preaching of the Swallow," give instruction based on the writings of Aristotle. When he tells the tale in its Scottish rural setting, the Narrator is acting as reader and teller of the fable, giving a reading which incorporates his own thoughts. The compassion which modifies his keen observation gives an effect which is beyond the "concrete and earthbound."

Throughout the fable series we find variations in the Narrator's moods and hence in the tone of the poem; assuming a different narrator for each would mean adding to the cast of narrators. We should, for instance, require one to deliver the formal "Prologue" to "The Lion and the Mouse" and another to learn from the foxes. Although she considers that the two voices have a unifying effect on the fable, which could otherwise be "schizoid" (Spanier, 1979–80: 124), Spanier implies that the narrators appear in turn, dividing between them the passages of thoughtful instruction and eyewitness description, surely a disruptive arrangement. The assumption of such extremes in the Narrator resembles those assumptions made about Henryson himself, and refuted in Fox's remarks about the poet's life:

> Henryson was neither an ignorant countryman, writing naïvely about animals, not a learned fifteenth-century humanist, abreast of all the latest intellectual development, although he has been variously pictured as each of these. Instead, he seems to have been a man of good general knowledge, but markedly unpedantic. (Fox, 1981: xxiv)

We may apply a similar judgement to what is revealed of the nature of Henryson's creation, the Narrator, who continually guides the presentation of the *Fables*.

The Narrator has now taken a position with the audience, and all the remaining fables are told from this point of view. He no longer appears to participate in any actions of the fable characters. Although his style makes his sympathies clear, he makes only a few direct comments in the tales, such as his proverbial utterance in "The Fox, the Wolf, and the Cadger," "He that of ressoun can not be content, / Bot couetis all, is abill all to tyne" (2189–2190), and the bitter conclusion to "The Wolf and the Lamb." In the last fable, "The Paddock and the Mouse," the description of the kite's taking of the toad and mouse ends "Off thair debait, thus quhen I hard outred" (2907), which could imply the Narrator's connection with the fable world. However, Fox posits that

> the text may be corrupt: one would expect something like *he had outred* . . . especially since it is suggested in line 2777 that the narrator was not himself an observer.   (Fox, 1981: 332)

Line 2777, the first of the tale, "Vpon ane tyme, as Esope culd report," does imply that the Narrator was not present; but we must remember that "The Two Mice," a tale in which the Narrator is an eyewitness, begins with a similar formula, "Esope, myne authour, makis mentioun" (162), and also includes the line "Bot I hard say scho passit to hir den" (358). Such evidence makes that of line 2777 seem less reliable. Still "I hard outred" does not necessarily indicate that the Narrator gained his information from a character rather than from his author, and the changing tone of the last stanzas of the tale more convincingly suggests detachment from it.

Throughout the tale, the preposterous adventures of the toad and mouse engage the audience's attention, beginning with the little mouse's incongruous misfortune of having no horse to ride across the stream. We follow every twist and turn of their discussions, with their arguments expressed as if the two were learned scholars. The two small creatures fill the stage, and gain an enormously exaggerated importance. The last moments of the tale bring an abrupt and shocking end to such a fantasy. The struggling animals are brutally but unemotionally caught by a natural enemy which swoops and carries them away "pyipand with mony pew" (2901), a phrase which faintly echoes the introduction of the little mouse "cryand with mony pietuous peip" (2783). The two protagonists, engaged in an unnatural conflict, are reduced to "scant . . . half ane fill" (2905) for a ravenous kite. Proportion and importance are restored with a jolt. The animal actors are revealed as insignificant shadows of the humans they represent, and the members of the audience are forced to direct their attention to real and human life. The Narrator has detached himself completely from the fable world, and advises listeners who want more information to ask those who saw the incidents "Giff this be trew, speir ʒe at thame that saw" (2909), casting doubt on its truth as he does so. How can we then take seriously the tiny creatures whose wrangling had absorbed our interest? The *moralitas* which follows is the most intimate in its addresses, with its first stanza beginning "my brother" (2910) and its last "Adew, my freind" (2969), and including the Narrator with his audience in the final prayer.

As we read the *Fables* then, we can trace a movement in the Narrator's purpose and in his site and point of view. He is at all times the reader of the works, relating them by contemporary references to his own time and place, adding to their immediacy and effect by the surprises of familiarly human thoughts and actions given incongruously to beasts. This function of reader is linked with that of teller of the tales, and he is the teacher of the moral lessons he draws. He is by no means an impartial observer or transmitter, since his own thoughts are revealed in the words and metaphors he chooses and in the interjections which occasionally give overt comment on the characters and their activities. This narrator is far from Flaubert's ideal of the author "like God in the universe, present everywhere and visible nowhere" (Steegmuller, 1980: 173). He uses cues to provoke responses from the audience, and the style of his telling may give a warning or induce pleasurable anticipation. The stories were old and well known long before Henryson retold them, but through his Narrator he adds surprises and freshness which prevent familiarity from dulling the sharpness of their teaching. The stern moralizing, so evident in the *moralitates*, does not rob the *Fables* of their interest and vigour. They could be delivered by an inconspicuous narrator, in impersonal fashion, but this manner would take away the immediacy given by the interaction of the Narrator and his assumed audience. This effect is felt even in a silent reading of the work. It is not written in epistolary style, as to a "gentle reader," but seems rather to be delivered from a desk or pulpit, to those who respond to tones of voice and mannerisms, implied in the idiosyncratic use of adjectives and repeated images. The illusion of the Narrator as eyewitness to some of the events adds to this effect and demands our attention.

As the *Fables* progress, we notice a change in the Narrator's point of view and prevailing mood. The central fables, "The Sheep and the Dog," "The Lion and the Mouse" and "The Preaching of the Swallow," show disturbances in the established sequence of tale and *moralitas* and in their telling. Significantly, the Narrator emphasizes his departure from a world which seems increasingly strange to him, to go home to the world of men. Here he stays, and, as he leaves the hopeful and fantastic realm of the lion, his tales become more tragic and their morals more gloomy. He does not desert man, however, to return to the happier place; and in the last fable he reduces it to an obvious fiction, in the dramatic conclusion which restores proportion to the audience, compelling concentration on the lessons of the tales and their application to human life. The Narrator's conclusions come to suggest that men alone cannot save themselves from their natures and the temptations they must face, and most of the latter fables end in a prayer for divine help or for happiness after death. "The Lion and the Mouse" is the last to anticipate much improvement in earthly life. The hard lessons are taught in fables which have tragic victims and savage humour, and although the Narrator seems generally to pity or despise man, he acknowledges that he belongs with him.

This progression is an ordered one, visible in the Bassandyne Print of the *Fables*, but unrevealed by the Bannatyne MS, with its interpolations and variations in order. It may be regarded then as additional evidence to support the case for the Bassandyne order and the notion of the *Fables* as a completed work, rather than a random or unfinished collection without plan or sequence (Burrow, 1975: 25). The juxtaposition of "The Cock and the Jasp" and "The Paddock and the Mouse," seen in the Bannatyne MS could sum up the lessons of all the fables, but the controlling sequence of varying moods and sites of the Narrator would be incompletely shown. Similarly, Bannatyne's choice to end his selection of Henryson's *Fables* with "The Lion and the Mouse" gives an optimistic conclusion which is at variance with the sadder and wiser frame of mind seen in the sequence of the Bassandyne Print.

We must wonder, since the two important versions end on such disparate notes, which of the two is to be preferred. Should we consider that the Narrator's mood is eventually hopeful or gloomily resigned, after his expositions of mankind's flaws? We may be answered by the evidence of continuing change in the Narrator's outlook. This can be seen in the Bassandyne order. There is a crescendo of optimism which leads from "The Cock and the Jasp," where so little harm comes to the protagonist that he is not even aware of his adventure, through the exploits of the fox and his companions, where there is justice for villains even if victims cannot escape, to the happiest of the *Fables*, "The Lion and the Mouse." In this group, only "The Sheep and the Dog" introduces a note of pessimism; and the obvious consequence of the sheep's loss of his wool in winter—his death—is anticipated in his speech but not seen, so that he does not appear to be an unavenged victim of injustice.

The remaining fables are increasingly gloomy. The birds to whom the swallow preaches wilfully ignore their means of salvation, and other victims are quite helpless. The lamb relies on the law, and the mouse and toad find that their intellect gives no defence. Other characters of this section—

the fox, the wolf, their human dupes and the foolish wether—inspire little sympathy. As the Narrator clearly shows, they are easily led to their misfortunes. The gathering pessimisim of the Narrator's mood is obvious, and shown in his increasing reliance on release from pain after death rather than reform during life, a change linked with his detachment from the tales to join his audience and express pronouncements as one of this group. This movement sustains the illusion of gathering truth for the world of the audience from the fanciful world of the tales. The abrupt restoration of scale in the last moments of "The Paddock and the Mouse" restores proportion and the significance of real beasts to real people. The Narrator can only be in the world of men, because he has closed the way to the fable world, leaving the audience without this distraction from the examination of their own lives. His presence does not permit any avoidance of this duty. He cannot be dismissed as a part of the fictitious world he has introduced, and his function is to instruct and remain with his audience, who think of him in the way posited by Leo Spitzer for the "I" found in medieval narrative:

> we must assume that the medieval public saw in the "poetic I"
> a representative of mankind, that it was interested only in this
> representative role of the poet.... It was a trifling matter who
> the empirical person behind this "I" actually was.
>
> (Spitzer, 1946: 415–416)

The Narrator, the "poetic I," has shown that he is a part of mankind, accepting, even if regretting, all that this implies.

VIII
Language, mood and order

Henryson's *Moral Fables*, when read in the order of the Bassandyne Print, reveal a continuing sequence of moral teaching and illustration, progressing from the general instruction to seek knowledge towards more particular duties to God and man. Several threads are repeated and eventually summarized in the last fable, "The Paddock and the Mouse," which allegorizes the struggle of the body and soul in the journey of life. We notice a change in the demeanour of the Narrator, as he leaves the just kingdom of the lion for the chaotic world of men, where pragmatism may overwhelm ideals. The progressive change can be traced, not only in the threads of narrative and the instruction given, but also in the Narrator's choice of topics and words which express his mood.

We find that some subjects, metaphors and words recur throughout the fable sequence, with varying emphasis, whereas some are associated only with particular sections of the *Fables*. An examination of these details gives a division of the *Fables*, in the Bassandyne order, into three parts: the early, confident section from "The Prologue" and "The Cock and the Jasp" to "The Trial of the Fox," concluding "And thus endis the talking of the tod" (1145); a central part with disturbing extremes of hope and despair, consisting of "The Sheep and the Dog," "The Lion and the Mouse" and "The Preaching of the Swallow," bounded by "And thus endis the preiching of the swallow" (1950); and the concluding section, where the Narrator's sombre mood of resigned acceptance of man is expressed in sad tales with touches of brutal humour and stern, detailed *moralitates*. The gross structure of these three sections, in the matter of themes and the interwoven threads of the *moralitates*, has already been discussed, as has the movement of the Narrator within the worlds of the characters and his audience. A closer inspection of his words confirms the idea of the progressive nature of telling the *Fables* in this order and the notion that the work is formed and complete, expressing, through the Narrator, the lessons which Henryson wanted to teach to mankind. Some thoughts recur throughout the work, and subsequent occurrences build on their first appearances. Indeed, some allusions would mean little without the first references, reinforcing the notion that the order used by Bassandyne is the one intended.

One of the recurring motifs is that of Fortune and her wheel. Medieval Christian doctrine did not dispel the hope and fear with which men regarded the Roman goddess Fortuna and the unpredictable twists of her wheel. The abrupt reversals seen throughout the *Fables* could suggest the influence of her capricious authority, and several particular references are made, most of them in the mouse fables. The "quhylis ... quhylis" construction, which evokes the spinning of the wheel, is introduced in "The Two Mice," and used with dramatic effect when it enhances the alarming picture of the helpless country mouse, being tossed about by the cat:

> Fra fute to fute he kest hir to and fra,
> Quhylis vp, quhylis doun, als tait as ony kid.
> Quhylis wald he lat hir rin vnder the stra;
> Quhylis wald he wink, and play with hir buk heid;
> Thus to the selie mous grit pane he did;
> Quhill at the last throw fair fortune and hap,
> Betwix the dosor and the wall scho crap.   (330–336)

Through this construction the passage is linked with earlier allusions to the mouse's haphazard way of life, "Richt soliter, quhyle vnder busk and breir, / Quhilis in the corne in vther mennis skaith" (166–167) and to the joyful meeting which changes her fortune, "quhylis thay leuch, and quhylis for ioy thay gret, / Quhyle kissit sweit, quhylis in armis plet" (193–194); it also anticipates her return to the countryside, "Quhylis throw the corne and quhylis throw the plane" (354). Reiteration serves to remind us of Fortune and her wheel in the struggles of the captured lion, "Welterand about with hideous rummissing, / Quhyle to, quhyle fra, quhill he mycht succour get" (1524–1525), and in those of the mouse and toad, "The mous vpwart, the paddok doun can pres; / Quhyle to, quhyle fra, quhyle doukit vp agane" (2891–2892). The *moralitates* of these fables give more direct comment. In his exposition of "The Lion and the Mouse," Aesop blames a lord's fall on "fals fortoun, quhilk of all variance / Is haill maistres, and leidar of the dance" (1604–1605); and the Narrator speaks at length of man's plight while his life is governed by the turning of Fortune's wheel, in the *moralitas* of "The Paddock and the Mouse":

> Now hie, now law, quhylis plungit vp, quhylis doun,
> Ay in perrell, and reddie for to droun;
>
> Now dolorus, now blyth as bird on breir;
> Now in fredome, now wardit in distres;
> Now haill and sound, now deid and brocht on beir;
> Now pure as Iob, now rowand in riches;
> Now gounis gay, now brats laid in pres;
> Now full as fische, now hungrie as ane hound;
> Now on the quheill, now wappit to the ground.   (2939–2947)

Fortune is suggested by the buckets in a well, found in Lowrence's impudent farewell to the wolf in "The Fox, the Wolf, and the Husbandman," "thus fairis it off fortoun: / As ane cummis vp, scho quheillis ane vther doun" (2418–2419). An unsteady ladder is mentioned in "The Wolf and the Wether," in the warning to the presumptuous:

> Out of thair cais in pryde thay clym sa hie
> That thay forbeir thair better in na steid,
> Quhill sum man tit thair heillis ouer thair heid   (2599–2601)

and in the closing lines of the *moralitas*:

> It settis na seruand for to vphald weir,
> Nor clym sa hie quhill he fall of the ledder:
> Bot think vpon the wolf and on the wedder.   (2613–2615)

The variations preserve the impression of uncontrollable and violent movement.

Another recurring motif is that of stripping away the outer covering, in a metaphorical or a literal sense. The Narrator introduces this thought in "The Prologue," in the metaphor of the kernel and the nutshell, a figure for a fable which carries a kernel of truth within its fictitious covering,

> The nuttis schell, thocht it be hard and teuch,
> Haldis the kirnell, sueit and delectabill;
> Sa lyis thair ane doctrine wyse aneuch
> And full of frute, vnder ane fenʒeit fabill.   (15–18)

The metaphor was frequently used in the period, and also implies the Narrator's purpose of exposing the lessons hidden in his tales and alerting the audience to look below the surface.

In its literal form, the motif is a gruesome one, appearing first in "The Fox and the Wolf," as a part of the goatherd's revenge on Lowrence, when "for his kid and vther violence, / He tuke his skyn and maid ane recompense" (773–774), leaving "his fatheris carioun, / Nakit, new slane" (811–812), to be found by Father-war. This fox seems wiser than his father when he rejects the offer of the mare to show her exemption, with the words: "Na, be Sanct Bryde! ... Me think it better / To sleip in haill nor in ane hurt skyn" (1029–1030). In "The Fox, the Wolf, and the Cadger," Lowrence is threatened with a similar misfortune, when the cadger plans his use of the fox's skin:

> 'Thair sall na pedder, for purs, nor ʒit for glufis,
> Nor ʒit for poyntis, pyke ʒour pellet fra me:
> I sall off it mak mittenis to my lufis

> Till hald my handis hait quhair euer I be;
> Till Flanderis sall it neuer saill the se.'   (2070–2074)

Little wonder that Lowrence runs from him, crying

> 'I hard quhat thou hecht to do with my skyn.
> Thy handis sall neuer in thay mittinnis tak heit,
> And thou wer hangit, carll, and all thy kyn!'   (2092–2094)

We should also recall the wolf's rash remark about his longing to be in the cadger's cart with the "nekhering," "Bot to be thair I wald gif all my clays" (2122). Lowrence escapes from this adventure with his life; but we realize that the sheep of "The Sheep and the Dog" will not be so fortunate. The loss of his fleece represents the losses inflicted on the poor by those in authority, mentioned by the sheep in the prayer overheard by the Narrator and reported in the *moralitas*. After such unjust treatment, "The pure is peillit" (1309). Even the sheep's enforced humility might not be sufficient for the lion, who upbraids the skittish mouse for dancing on him:

> 'I put the cace, I had bene deid or slane,
> And syne my skyn bene stoppit full off stra;
> Thocht thow had found my figure lyand swa,
> Because it bare the prent off my persoun,
> Thow suld for feir on kneis haue fallin doun.'   (1449–1453)

The stripping of the landscape by the wild winds of winter brings the first intimation of discord into the Narrator's account of ordered creation in the first part of "The Preaching of the Swallow," disrupting the atmosphere of fruitful autumn,

> Syne wynter wan, quhen austerne Eolus,
> God off the wynd, with blastis boreall
> The grene garment off somer glorious
> Has all to-rent and reuin in pecis small.   (1692–1695)

The unwise birds eventually die in this harsh, bare season, driven by their desperate hunger to the fowler's chaff and nets. In "The Wolf and the Wether," the foolish shepherd is easily persuaded to clothe the wether in the skin of his dead dog. The last use of the motif is part of the restoration of reality in "The Paddock and the Mouse," the grim, impersonal act of the kite's flaying of the toad and mouse, his natural prey, "And bellieflaucht full fettislie thame fled" (2904).

Thus the literal references to skinning and stripping carry at least the threat of death, and we see a change in the creatures affected as the *Fables* proceed. Justice prevails in the early fables, and the goatherd takes

Lowrence's skin as a recompense for injury. Later, death threatens and may come to milder, harmless animals, while the fox escapes to do more mischief. The torn landscape of winter keeps the birds from their salvation when they can find no food but the chaff in the fowler's snare. Finally, the stripping of the toad's and mouse's skins is only a part of the process by which the kite preys on his natural food; and the lines describing this event are part of the Narrator's restoration of perspective which forces members of his audience to examine their own lives. The associations change as the fables are told, and echo the change in mood of the Narrator, from that of one who has confidence in justice to one who finds man incorrigible and the law ineffective.

Two themes which recur as significant metaphors for man's condition are those of blindness and bondage, in physical and spiritual senses. Literal instances of blindness are found in Chantecleir's closing of his eyes (473, 477), Lowrence's pretence of infirmity when he is summoned before the lion (967, 995), and the genuine blindness of the mole (916). Bondage is seen in the capture of the country mouse (329), of the lion and mouse of "The Lion and the Mouse" (1522, 1418), and of the birds of "The Preaching of the Swallow" (1873), and the binding of the mouse and toad in "The Paddock and the Mouse" (2874). Although the consequences of these circumstances may be grave, it is clear that spiritual blindness and bondage are regarded more seriously. The Narrator first raises the issue in "The Two Mice," when he speaks of "Grit aboundance and blind prosperitie" (377), and his remarks are more specific in "The Preaching of the Swallow," when he describes the plight of the soul:

> Thairfoir our saull with sensualitie
> So fetterit is in presoun corporall,
> We may not cleirlie vnderstand nor se
> God as he is, nor thingis celestiall;
> Our mirk and deidlie corps materiale
> Blindis the spirituall operatioun,
> Lyke as ane man wer bundin in presoun.   (1629–1635)

The tale which follows shows the wilful blindness of the birds which results in their gruesome capture in the fowler's net. The *moralitas* speaks of the parting of the soul and body, a theme of "The Paddock and the Mouse," where the binding of the two is dramatically illustrated in the rash act of the mouse,

> This lytill mous, heir knit thus be the schyn,
> The saull of man betakin may in deid—
> Bundin, and fra the bodie may not twyn,
> Quhill cruell deith cum brek of lyfe the threid.   (2948–2951)

In the later fables, the welfare of the soul is of greater concern to the Narrator than is the earthly life of the body, which appears eventually to be a loathsome and degrading encumbrance. This attitude, introduced in "The Sheep and the Dog," is resolved in "The Paddock and the Mouse." The sheep's prayer for the poor, "sen that we ar opprest / In to this eirth, grant vs in heuin gude rest" (1319–1320), takes a more general form:

> Now Christ for vs that deit on the rude,
> Of saull and lyfe as thow art Saluiour,
> Grant vs till pas in till ane blissit hour.   (2973–2975)

The implication that an improvement in earthly life must be forgotten in favour of the aspirations of the soul suggests an increasingly gloomy opinion of mankind's life in its physical form, the body.

A similar gradation may be seen in the references to play. These begin with the Narrator's bland approval in "The Prologue,"

> And clerkis sayis, it is richt profitabill
> Amangis ernist to ming ane merie sport,
> To blyth the spreit and gar the tyme be schort   (19–21)

and later, "With sad materis sum merines to ming / Accordis weill" (26–27). We see that "merines" does not necessarily gain approval through the sour suggestion that the jasp may have been swept out by "damisellis wantoun and insolent / That fane wald play and on the streit be sene" (71–72); and we learn from "The Two Mice" that trouble may come to spoil light-heartedness rather than the happier reverse of this process:

> Swa intermellit is aduersitie
> With eirdlie ioy, swa that na state is frie
> Without trubill or sum vexatioun.   (368–370)

Play develops sinister connotations, and "merines" may come from the uneasy enjoyment of the dramatic account of the cat's play with the country mouse or from a vicious joke at the expense of the despised wolf. Lowrence shows commendable composure when he is pierced by the goatherd's arrow and warns "Me think na man may speik ane word in play, / Bot now on dayis in ernist it is tane" (770–771). His son, Father-war, is one "That luifit weill with pultrie to tig and tar" (802). This fox's notion of play extends to his attempt to hide in the court of the lion, where "[h]e playit bukhude behind, fra beist to beist" (970), and to his dealings with a lamb, after which he claims: "My purpois wes with him for to haif plaid" (1079). Even the dull-witted wolf suspects the fox's intentions when they search for the mythical cheese in "The Fox, the Wolf, and the Husbandman," shown in his words: "Lowrence, thou playis bellie blind; / We seik all nycht, bot na thing can we find" (2383–2384).

The fox's villainy is distinguished by its artistic efficiency and wit, and his graceful performance does seem to be play rather than effort. The wolf is a brutal and inept evil-doer, and the idea of play enrages him. This is viciously illustrated when the foolish wether offers his explanation for pursuing the wolf, "Maister . . . bot to haue playit with ȝow" (2558). The filthy wolf finds nothing playful about the terrifying chase, and the wether's attempt to excuse his behaviour has no more success than the fox's use of this ruse in "The Trial of the Fox" (1079). The lamb's attempt to justify his drinking from the same stream also infuriates the wolf. His reply to the lamb's mild scriptural argument is "Ȝaa! . . . Ȝit pleyis thow agane?" (2671). The last comment on play is made in the mouse's sadly prophetic reply to the toad's explanation of the method for helping her to swim, "To preif that play, it wer our perrillous!" (2860). Play, as the *Fables* advance, moves far from amusement to enliven the task of learning, to be linked with cruelty, desperation and danger. This movement is another indication of the change in the Narrator's mood.

The Narrator refers several times to the association of evil with darkness, ironically often by ascribing human intentions to the natural behaviour of nocturnal creatures. The association is introduced in the disapproving comment made about the country mouse who lives "Withoutin fyre or candill birnand bricht, / For comonly sic pykeris luffis not lycht" (202–203). As the tales are told, the Narrator frequently connects the shadowy, changing light with Lowrence and his mischief. The fox is first seen, lying in wait for Chantecleir, "in to the gray dawing" (427), and after the chase and the cock's escape, Lowrence must hide, because he

> durst na mair with miching intermell
> Als lang as leme or licht wes off the day,
> Bot bydand nicht full styll lurkand he lay. (618–620)

When he emerges he still shuns the light, looking out cautiously, "[a]nd kest his hand vpon his ee on hicht, / Merie and glade that cummit wes the nicht" (626–627).

The linking of darkness and evil is familiar and general, and Lowrence's case is a particular example, which the Narrator repeats with variations such as the fox's discomfort in daylight, both at the court of the lion, when "Phebus with his bemis / Consumit had the mistie cluddis gray" (866–867), and, when he is summoned as a witness to the husbandman's unintended vow, "Lowrence come lourand, for he luifit neuer licht" (2294), together with the enjoyable irony of the exclamation to his confessor, the wolf, "Ȝe ar the lanterne and the sicker way / Suld gyde sic sempill folk as me to grace" (677–678). The fox is quite at his ease in moonlight, when he leads the wolf to search for the great cheese.

The doubtful, shadowy evening "Quhen Hesperus to schaw his face began" (1173), is recognized by the innocent sheep of "The Sheep and the Dog" as a dangerous time to plead before the consistory court. His brave words, "Heir I declyne the iuge, the tyme, the place" (1187), have no effect, but confirm the association which has been stressed by the Narrator. The economy of references made in the latter sections of the work suggests that they are intended to augment the earlier instances, and Lowrence's almost complete monopoly of the motif encourages the audience to expect him to appear from the shadows.

In contrast, the fable which celebrates optimism and shows the rewards of good deeds, "The Lion and the Mouse," begins with a prologue filled with brilliant sunshine. This fable is the core of the work, the middle one of the three that form the central section of the *Fables*. Each is told, at least in part, through the Narrator's experiences. Here, the first, confident expectations of the work are disturbed and grow pessimistic, with similar disturbances in the arrangement of the tales and their *moralitates*, and the Narrator moves from the world of fable characters to accept his place with mankind.

The time of the "Prologue" to "The Lion and the Mouse," which is noted with unusual precision, "In middis of Iune" (1321), "In ane mornyng betuix mid day and nicht" (1325), and the balanced numbers of stanzas before and after the fable suggest a mid-point in the fable sequence as well as the middle of the season. Balance in the fable itself is implied in the juxtaposition of the two protagonists, the greatest and least in the animal kingdom, and in their neatly matched adventures in which each rescues the other from captivity. The fable represents the ideal—that a character should learn a lesson, be changed by it and then rewarded for making the improvement. It marks the peak of optimism in the *Fables*, framed by those fables which first express doubt in justice and happy endings. The central fables pay closest attention to the settings of the tales, stressing the bleakness of the countryside of "The Sheep and the Dog," the beautiful unreality of the landscape in which the Narrator dreams in "The Lion and the Mouse" and the details of the changing scene in "The Preaching of the Swallow." "The Lion and the Mouse" is the core around which the other fables are arranged, and those which precede it are found to differ in tone and the nature of their ideas when compared with those which follow. This comparison may be extended to the details of expression shown in the Narrator's choice of words and images, and the changing stress and sense of his diction traces the same progress in mood and tone which has been observed in the use of motif. The changing use of images and ideas contributes to the effects achieved and the darkening texture of thought.

We may consider the adjectives "gentil" and "iolie," with their pleasant, light-hearted associations and, in contrast, the more sober considerations of "selie" and "pure," together with the Narrator's continual attention to the soul and its welfare. "Gentil" and "iolie" suggest a way of life which is above mundane considerations. It is not surprising that both words are first used in the *Fables* to describe the beautiful jasp, the jewel symbolizing the knowledge which can elevate all men to a plane beyond the sordid concerns which must engage the foolish cock. The jasp is both "gentill" (79, 110, 127) and "iolie" (62, 69, 120). The two mice can enjoy light-hearted pleasure; their fable refers to "ane gentill hart" (234) and "all their iolitie" (292), but introduces the sinister presence of "Gib Hunter, our iolie cat" (326). The handsome cock of "The Cock and the Fox" is also associated with elegance, and he is described as "ane iolie cok" (415) and "gentill Chantecleir" (410, 434, 487). Lowrence wishes to lead a gracious life by any means within his power. When he attempts to justify his methods, he confesses: "I eschame to thig, I can not wirk, ʒe wait, / ʒit wald I fane pretend to gentill stait" (710–711). Both adjectives are used formally in the description of the animals which bow before the lion, including "[t]he iolie ionet, and the gentill steid" (898). The humbler sheep's despair may be summarized in his words, "Gentrice is slane, and pietie is ago" (1312).

These words and their usual associations accord with the formal, aureate diction of the "Prologue" to "The Lion and the Mouse," set in "that ioly sweit seasoun" (1321). Aesop announces "I am off gentill blude" (1370), an idea unlike the traditional one that he was a slave, and he is addressed by the Narrator as "gentill schir" (1398). The concept of "gentilesse" is considered twice by the admirable mouse of the fable: first when she pleads her unworthiness to be eaten by one "[v]ont till be fed with gentill vennesoun" (1495), and later when she rescues the lion, saying

'Now wer I fals and richt vnkynd
Bot gif I quit sumpart thy gentilnes
Thow did to me.'   (1547–1549)

The words are suited to "The Preaching of the Swallow" in the formal, general description of the coming of "somer with his iolie mantill grene" (1678) and "Phebus, with his goldin bemis gent" (1682), and in the particular case of the Narrator's journey, in "Iune, that iolie tyde" (1776). But these adjectives, associated with lightness, grace and nobility, have no place in the fables which follow "The Preaching of the Swallow," and do not occur except for one argument of the wily toad, who defends her unwholesome appearance by asserting "Wer I als fair as iolie Absolon, / I am no causer off that grit beutie" (2842–2843).

In contrast, we may look at words with connotations far from courtly life—"selie" and "pure"—words which generally describe the victims in the *Fables*. The dwelling of the country mouse, "ane semple wane, / Off fog and farne" (197-198), is called "[a]ne sillie scheill" (199), and this is the only use of the adjective for an inanimate object. Elsewhere it describes the most helpless characters of the tales: the mice of "The Two Mice" (204, 299, 334) the mouse of "The Paddock and the Mouse" (2784, 2893), and the hens of "The Cock and the Fox" (492). It is most frequently associated with sheep characters: the sheep of "The Sheep and the Dog" (1170, 1258), the sheep (and the shepherd) of "The Wolf and the Wether" (2467, 2470), and the most innocent of victims, the lamb of "The Wolf and the Lamb" (2620, 2625, 2637, 2700). Only once is the word used light-heartedly, when Lowrence asks Freir Wolff Waitskaith for an easy penance, "To set ... [his] selie saull in way off grace" (722).

There is a similar pattern in the use of "pure" and references to "pouertie." The first character of the *Fables*, the cock, is described as "Richt cant and crous, albeit he was bot pure" (65), but the Narrator pays more attention to his intellectual and spiritual deficiencies than his lack of material possessions. The country mouse is pleased to assert "I keip the ryte and custome off my dame, / And off my syre, levand in pouertie" (215-216). Similarly, the "men of contemplatioun" (1111), represented by the grey mare, live "[a]bstractit from this warldis wretchitnes, / In wilful pouertee, fra pomp and pryde" (1115-1116). Such early references do not carry painful implications, but hint that poverty is to be admired as a rejection of the world's temptations rather than dreaded as a factor which can make lives wretched and helpless, just as "selie" is used in early fables of characters who can be lucky or resourceful although they have slight physical strength or power. We find, too, that Lowrence speaks of the poverty encountered in the uncertain life of a thief, "For euer we steill and euer alyk ar pure" (659), although his brief remorse is not to be taken seriously.

Poverty must be a serious issue for the victims in later fables, a category from which we may exempt the "siluer-seik" (2036) wolf of "The Fox, the Wolf, and the Cadger," and the dog who called the sheep before the consistory court "because that he wes pure" (1147). We may judge how gravely the topic is considered by the frequency with which "pure" occurs in the *moralitates* of these fables. The poor are shown to be victims in the *moralitas* of "The Sheep and the Dog," in the words of the Narrator (1259, 1268) and in those of the shorn sheep (1303, 1309, 1318). The Narrator sternly warns that "riches of array / Will cause pure men presumpteous for to be" (2595-2596), in the *moralitas* of "The Wolf and the Wether," but he speaks with pity in that of "The Wolf and the Lamb," of "The pure pepill ... Of quhome the lyfe is half ane purgatorie" (2707-2709). Here he addresses those who are "oppressouris of pure men" (2712), those who "will not thoill in pece ane pureman be" (2731), speaking in some detail of their offences against such victims as "the pure husband" (2737). The Narrator declares "for ane bud the pure man he ouerthrawis" (2718) and that "it cryis ane vengeance vnto the heuinnis hie / To gar ane pure man wirk but meit or fe" (2761–2762), vehemently concluding:

> O thow grit lord, that riches hes and rent,
> Be nocht ane wolf, thus to deuoir the pure!
> . . . .
> For till oppress, thow sall haif als grit pane
> As thow the pure with thy awin hand had slane.
>
> (2763–2769)

Little remains to be said of poverty after this *moralitas*. The Narrator simply includes "Now pure as Iob, now rowand in riches" (2944) among the upheavals of a life governed by Fortune's wheel. Only two references are made to poverty in the tales of the central and later fables, each by a character who enjoys some success. The mouse of "The Lion and the Mouse" pleads her "simple pouertie" (1435), contrasting it with the lion's "mychtie hie magnyfycence" (1436), and the fox, laughing, asks "Wald I tak it vpon my conscience / To do sa pure a man as ʒone offence?" (2348–2349) before he gives a judgement in the husbandman's favour. The fox, in this case, is shown to be "the Feind" (2431), and the wolf is identified as "ane wickit man / Quhilk dois the pure oppres in euerie place" (2427–2428). The less sombre references do not diminish the serious tone of the Narrator's words. Rather, the mouse illustrates helplessness when she is trapped in the lion's paw and the fox's maliciously joking question suggests further deception and exploitation of those who are already weak.

The growing dejection of the Narrator's mood is expressed in his thoughts about the soul. It is mentioned throughout the *Fables*, and, as in the case of other recurring themes, the references become more serious as the Narrator proceeds. The first allusions are in the enthusiastic declaration of the benefits of the jasp, "To mannis saull it is eternall meit" (140) and in the admonition, "Haif we richis, na better lyfe we bid, / Of science thocht the saull be bair and blind" (157–158). Most references to the soul in the early fables are not gloomy. The phrase "be my saull" is used as a mild oath, to give emphasis to the town mouse's disapproval of her sister's simple fare when she exclaims "Na, be my saull, I think it bot ane scorne" (211), and a pretence of respectability to Lowrence's flattery of Chantecleir, "Schir, be my saull, ʒe neid not be effraid" (436) and "Schir, be my saull, and the blissit sacrament, / My hart warmys, me think I am at hame"(455–456). The phrase is also used by the mouse in "The Lion and the Mouse" (1445), the husbandman in "'The Fox, the Wolf, and the Husbandman" (2263) and the lamb in "The Wolf and the Lamb" (2640). The fox's remarks to the wolf as his confessor, about the care of his "selie saull" (722), and to the wolf as his dupe in "The Fox, the Wolf, and the Husbandman," protesting "Schir, trow ӡe not I haue ane saull to keip?" (2363), may be considered with a cynicism similar to Lowrence's.

The Narrator's direct references to the soul are far from cynical. Taking the example of the fox whose misdeeds serve only to benefit his heir, he condemns man, in the tale of "The Trial of the Fox," in the following strong terms:

> O fulische man! Plungit in wardlynes
> To conqueis wrangwis guidis, gold and rent,
> To put thy saull in pane or heuines,
> To riche thy air.   (831–834)

He gives much importance to the matter of the soul in the introductory section of "The Preaching of the Swallow," using metaphors of blindness and bondage to explain its weaknesses:

> Thairfoir our saull with sensualitie
> So fetterit is in presoun corporall,   (1629–1630)

> In *Metaphisik* Aristotell sayis
> That mannis saull is lyke ane bakkis ee,
> ....
> Hir ene ar waik, the sone scho may not se:
> Sa is our saull with fantasie opprest,
> To knaw the thingis in nature manifest.   (1636–1642)

His conclusion in this passage is that

> God is in his power infinite,
> And mannis saull is febill and ouer small
> Off vnderstanding waik and vnperfite.   (1643–1645)

The conclusions of the *moralitas* are severe and exact. Here we are told of the sowing of "poysoun and mony wickit thocht / In mannis saull, quhilk Christ full deir hes bocht" (1900–1901) and of their growth "quhen the saull, as seid in to the eird, / Geuis consent in delectatioun" (1902–1903). Death brings a grim separation:

> Allace, quhat cair, quhat weiping is and wo,
> Quhen saull and bodie partit ar in twane!
> The bodie to the wormis keitching go,
> The saull to fyre, to euerlestand pane.   (1930–1933)

The *moralitas* of "The Paddock and the Mouse" gives a more complete exposition of this parting and of the struggling of the body with the soul, where "This lytill mous ... The saull of man betakin may in deid" (2948–2949), and

> The watter is the warld, ay welterand
> With mony wall of tribulatioun,
> In quhilk the saull and bodye wer steirrand,
> Standand distinyt in thair opinioun:
> The spreit vpwart, the body precis doun;
> The saull rycht fane wald be brocht ouer, I wis,
> Out of this warld into the heuinnis blis.   (2955–2961)

The Narrator's concern is shown in his concluding prayer to "Christ for vs that deit on the rude, / Of saull and lyfe as thow art Saluiour" (2973–2974). Thus the allusions to the soul progress from unthinking evocation and jaunty irreverence to a consideration even more serious than that given to the benefits of the jasp. The Narrator stresses its welfare and implies the possibility of damnation. His purpose is to encourage his audience to care for the soul, preferring this consideration to that of improvement in earthly life, where the hope of justice often seems remote.

His varying use of the words mentioned indicates his changing mood, as it passes from confidence and optimism to a resigned acceptance of incorrigible humanity. Whereas the Narrator's mood sets the tone for the whole work, the characters have an important influence within the fables. We may consider the sheep's sorrowful prayers, which introduce the note of pessimism and the swallow's preaching which confirms this, remembering that both these creatures may be temporary substitutes for the Narrator. More important than either is the fox, and we notice how often his flippant remarks introduce topics which the Narrator treats solemnly. The welfare of the soul is an example. When he has some anxiety, after casting his horoscope, Lowrence asks his confessor for guidance. Such direction is surely the province of a figure such as the Narrator, and we may laugh or gasp at the thought of the wolf as a spiritual guide. The suggestion is a part of the Narrator's ironic approach, and we see that, although the truth may be manipulated, in the early fables justice will prevail. This attitude ends with "The Trial of the Fox," and the point is clearly marked by the last line of its *moralitas*, "And thus endis the talking of the tod" (1145). From that point we see that justice is not freely available, even in a court of law. The next fable, "The Sheep and the Dog," shows this with sad clarity.

The three central fables, each with a disturbance in the expected order of tale and *moralitas*, demonstrate the dislocation of man's society and institutions and neglect of temporal and spiritual duties which lead to a loss of hope. The unreality of the core of the work, "The Lion and the Mouse," is emphasized by its being told in a dream by a remote figure who has little confidence in its success. The next fable, "The Preaching of the Swallow," has a realistic background in the Narrator's experience of the natural cycle of the seasons, and the story is told with sadly realistic imagery. This section concludes with the words, "And thus endis the preiching of the swallow" (1950). It is followed by tales of the fox which emphasize the cynical injustice of the world, easily manipulated by a character such as Lowrence. The atmosphere extends to "The Wolf and the Wether" which tells of the hopeless efforts of a foolish upstart, and the tragic tale of "The Wolf and the Lamb" which enhances the scale of "The Sheep and the Dog" in the injustice of the story and contrast between its protagonists. In "The Paddock and the Mouse" all the lessons of the previous fables are summarized in the struggles of mouse and toad, soul and body.

The progressively changing tone gives further evidence for accepting the Bassandyne order of the *Fables*. The tone is set by the changing pattern of ideas and the attitudes held as they are discussed; and may be traced in the use and frequency of words and concepts used by the Narrator. The jauntiness of the fox gives way to the sorrowful acceptance of the Narrator, as he tells tales with increasingly dismal outcomes, using words with serious associations, removed from those of the earlier fables, and turns his attention from the possibility of earthly happiness to the care of the soul.

IX
The journey of life

The Narrator's last fable, "The Paddock and the Mouse," is the point to which all his reading, telling and teaching lead. Here he gives us, his audience, his reading of a fable which other authors told for a different purpose. His telling of the story takes all his themes to their conclusions and the explicit teaching of the *moralitas* draws together and includes all the lessons of previous fables. In this feat, Henryson achieves the art of the fabulist as it is conceived by Douglas Gray, which "consists in finding a balance of opposites—sympathy and detachment, comedy and tragedy, in creating his constantly shifting world" (Gray, 1979: 113).

It is assumed that Henryson used as his source the fable briefly told by Gualterus Anglicus, Walter the Englishman, *De Mure et Rana*, the tale of a mouse and a frog, which suggests that those with evil intentions will not escape punishment; his reading of the fable alters the scale, complexity and moral of the earlier version (Bastin, 1930: 9–10). Walter's protagonists are two creatures of similar size and consequence to man, and the kite is an opportunist predator. His version conveys little of the studied wickedness of the toad's deceptive persuasion and of the struggles of the mouse whose eagerness makes her susceptible.

The Narrator offers a reading which increases the depravity of the villain by telling of the larger, less appealing toad, and enhances the helplessness of the victim. The elaborations of character and dialogue suggest a greater contrast in the nature of the two protagonists. The argument between the two characters gives an illustration of the danger of trusting in knowledge and accepted truths which surpasses the experiences of other innocents of the *Fables*, and develops the lion's comment that "The greitest clerkis ar not the wysest men" (1064). The Narrator's *moralitas* draws together the lessons which precede it, before advancing to his image of life.

The Narrator leads his audience in a journey through the *Fables* to reach a tale which he tells as an allegory of life. Paradoxically he chooses his most preposterous tale to reveal the fundamental truth that man's life is governed by the conflicting influences of his body and soul, and he illustrates these forces in the incongruous yoking of the toad and mouse. No tale could be more absurd than this one, from which he draws his final teaching. The two protagonists of "The Paddock and the Mouse" have no conceivable connection. It is, by contrast, not difficult to imagine the association of rogues seen in the fox and wolf fables, or that of predator and victim in the pairing of cock and fox or wolf and lamb. Neither toad nor mouse can gain anything from the other in natural life, and even in the fictitious context of the tale, the advantage which each expects seems improbable. How can we suppose that the mouse will be transported across the stream, or, more alarmingly, that the toad will gain from murdering a harmless creature which could not even be prey? Through the toad's unprovoked and unreasoning hatred, the problem of motiveless evil is implied, even if it is not explicitly addressed.[1]

It is much easier to imagine the situations of "The Lion and the Mouse," where two strangely assorted characters work for mutual advantages which can readily be appreciated. In "The Lion and the Mouse" each protagonist saves the other, and both live, having learned a lesson; in "The Paddock and the Mouse," one tries to destroy the other and both die. When captives are freed in "The Lion and the Mouse," they are released to a better life, but "The Paddock and the Mouse" describes a kind of bondage which can be ended only by death. The central fable, "The Lion and the Mouse," is told in an optimistic dream, but "The Paddock and the Mouse" jolts the audience back to earthly life with only the comfort of the hope of happiness after death.

The two creatures, preposterously but inextricably linked, are used by the Narrator to give his last message, fixing in the mind of his audience an image of life which is both ludicrous and pathetic, summarizing all the teaching of the earlier fables. We have already looked at his style of telling, with the discernment shown in the readings he offers the audience, and at his way of teaching through direct address and the implications of repeated references. In the last fable all the methods are used, as the Narrator completes his detachment from the imaginary world of the tales and reduces it to an illusion, while he extracts the moral lesson which is at the core of all his teaching. He tells us that throughout life, the aspiring soul must live with the corruptible body. In the tale, when both creatures become food for the kite, and a natural hunger is only partly satisfied, there is no suggestion of any emotion or moral decision. Rather, the Narrator describes the actions of a natural bird of prey and brings moral decision back to the world of his audience of reasoning people, where it must belong.

The enforced yoking of the body and soul is the source of every moral dilemma which man must face. In the ridiculous picture of the two struggling creatures, in surroundings which are natural to one but alien to the other, the Narrator has presented a bizarre image of life. The conflict of the

---

[1] The toad is described as a poisonous symbol of envy by Robert Pope (Pope, 1979: 463–464). He also comments on Henryson's changes to Walter's version of the fable and advances reasons for considering the paddock to be a toad rather than a frog (Pope, 1979: 461, 462).

aspiring soul, almost overcome by the vicious body, illustrates the continuing battle of good and evil. It is not as difficult to consider the ludicrous wranglings of an engagingly foolish heroine and an obviously evil adversary as it is to confront the theological issue of the incompatibility of spirit and flesh. The fable is more engaging than a sermon—it does "blyth the spreit" (21)—and it is saved from complete bleakness by the toad's failure to overcome the mouse before the kite claims them and the Narrator's willingness to join the human audience whose failings he has exposed. All the temptations to baseness, exemplified in the deeds of such characters as the fox, the wolf or the foolish birds, are summarized in the urgent need of the toad to overwhelm the susceptible mouse. The binding of the two creatures and the variations in the toad's methods of persuasion demonstrate the inevitability and diversity of the soul's encounters with evil. These impressions are strengthened by the place of this fable in the series, after the preparation of earlier themes and images which are recalled in references to Fortune, bondage and the wilful blindness of self-deception experienced by the mouse, encouraged by the deliberate deceit of the toad.

The toad's reasoning is still more proficient than the spurious arguments of the fox, because her victim can recognize the wickedness revealed in her appearance. The mouse even retreats from the toad, crying "Giff I can ony skill of phisnomy, / Thow hes sumpart of falset and inuy" (2824–2825). The toad's method of deception is the one seen in other fables. She manipulates her dupe's eagerness by telling the mouse what she wants to hear. We can recognize the style of deception used on Chantecleir and the wolf, but those victims were not as perceptive. This mouse represents a soul which has received instruction. The toad is the most brazen of the deceivers in the *Fables*; no other would speak

> 'Off silkin toung and cheir rycht amorous,
> With mynd inconstant, fals, and wariand,
> Full of desait and menis cautelous.' (2848–2850)

Although the toad is so obviously wicked, she is full of convincing reasons for being considered harmless and benevolent, being able to cite authorities and disclaim any responsibility for her evil physiognomy. Her arguments suggest the plausible temptations which continually try the soul, for which the mouse makes an endearing figure. Her longings for a better life are ironically expressed as an urge to eat sweeter food, the kind of longing for which the town mouse is censured in the second fable.

The dialogue of the toad and mouse is revealed in the *moralitas* to be a dialogue of the body and soul. Since the speakers do not perceive themselves to represent these entities, there are no specific references in their speeches, but there are resemblances to other dialogues of this kind, seen in the fear and hatred which are expressed.[2] The mouse is repelled by the ugliness of the toad, just as the soul rejects the one addressed as "*pou* fekele flessch" in speeches of contempt for the corruptible, decaying body.[3] The debate of the toad and mouse takes the discussion beyond mere contempt for the body, and even further than the mutual accusations of body and soul which we find in "A disputeson between the body and the sowle." In "The Paddock and the Mouse," the evil toad attempts to show herself as helpful and gracious to the mouse, in the misleading description of her swimming, and her offer to

> 'find the way,
> Withoutin hors, brig, boit, or ʒit galay,
> To bring ʒow ouer saiflie, be not afeird—
> And not wetand the campis off ʒour beird.'   (2801–2804)

She also presents herself as a victim of her uncaused appearance. Most tellingly, she plays on the mouse's fault of unreasonable greed, so that flaws are exposed in both creatures. In this unconscious debate between body and soul, we may find closer resemblances to Marvell's "A Dialogue between the Soul and Body," where each speaker bitterly condemns the faults of the other. The binding which brings the mouse the loss of "baith lyfe and libertie" (2863) which she dreads is echoed in the confinement of the soul "[w]ith bolts of Bones, that fetter'd stands / In Feet; and manacled in Hands."[4] The mutual plight of the two is confirmed in the body's reply: "O who shall me deliver whole / From bonds of this Tyrannic Soul?"[5]

Henryson's grotesque picture continues the tradition of such debates, linking the earlier medieval forms with the Renaissance work. The two creatures demonstrate the opposition of characters who are neither entirely good nor altogether evil. The toad and mouse share a common ground of intellect, and each can argue with confidence, but the toad gains the upper hand because she is admirably clever whereas the mouse is engagingly skittish. Their premortal dialogue of body and soul has more in common with Marvell's poem than with the comminatory style of the thirteenth century. The image of life as the wrangling of two such creatures has the startling quality of a metaphysical conceit, presenting the fundamental

---

[2] For example those collected by Carleton Brown: "Shroud and Grave," "Doomsday," "The Latemest Day" (Brown, 1971: 31, 42, 44, 46, 50) and "A disputeson between the body and the sowle" (Varnhagen, 1963: 229–244).

[3] "A disputeson between the body and the sowle," line 14.

[4] "A Dialogue between the Soul and the Body," lines 3–4 (Margoliouth, 1927: 20–21). Kitty Scoular Datta suggests that Marvell's poem closely resembles a poem of Hermann Hugo in *Pia Desideria* (Antwerp, 1624), a Latin work of wide circulation in its original form and in translation (Datta, 1969).

[5] Marvell, "A Dialogue between the Soul and the Body,' lines 11–12.

problem of existence in the bizarre form of a journey to be ridiculed pitied—with life reduced to a struggle between oddly assorted oppc which cannot be won by either contender. Mortal life must involve both soul and body; although neither can be victorious, neither can be defeated and death will take both. The toad's response to the mouse's cries illustrates the paradox that the soul's wishes must be formed while it is contained within the body. Man, in life, can have the aspiring, confident innocence seen in the mouse, balanced by the calculating wickedness of the toad, but neither of these can completely overwhelm the other, expressed in the image which also suggests Fortune's caprice: "The mous vpwart, the paddock doun can pres; / Quhyle to, quhyle fra, quhyle doukit vp agane" (2891–2892).

Although this picture may be acceptable when an unvarnished exposition of man's dilemma would be insufferable, it is clear that the Narrator cannot leave his audience with the thought that life is merely pitifully amusing. His message is not trivial and he intends to enforce his fables with inescapable teachings. Although he despises the fleshly tendencies of man, symbolized in the loathsome form of the toad, he retains pity and gentle ridicule for the frail and foolish soul in the animal disguise which he has previously treated with affection. He retains this feeling for the soul which "fane wald be brocht ouer ... Out of this warld into the heuinnis blis" (2960–2961), and in conclusion he allies himself with the soul's aspirations, commending himself and the audience to Christ.

The journey is done, and we, the readers, have been carried along in the illusion that we have joined the audience for whom the Narrator has produced a reading of the *Fables* of Aesop, telling us the tales and teaching us the lessons, allowing us to face aspects of human life through the adventures of fictitious animals and insisting that we do so. The Narrator has cajoled, enlightened, bullied, pitied and admonished, using fanciful tales and conventionally stern moralizing. His teachings are the familiar Christian ones of duty to God and man, but the *Moral Fables* have innovations and conclusions which may surprise. The work forms a unified whole, balanced about an optimistic yet sadly unrealistic central fable, with hopeful early stories but a gathering realization of the possibility of persistent sorrow, and the Narrator shows the frame of mind described by Matthew McDiarmid (when writing of Henryson) as

> a personality much less at peace, a much more demanding and challenging mind, neither quite at home in his own Christian world nor easily accommodated to the taste of our materialistic one.   (McDiarmid, 1977: 28)

The Narrator himself must balance his audience's world of reality with illusion, that of the tales, and eventually he chooses to join and remain with the audience, in steps which may be traced in the order of the *Fables* seen in the Bassandyne Print, as may the development of his themes. Members of the audience are taken from the level of perception shown by the cock in the first fable to a point where illusion may be dismissed, and they may try to apprehend the lessons of this world while hoping for the benefits of the next. This journey depends on the guidance of Henryson's creation, the Narrator.

Appendix

Order in manuscript witnesses for the
Moral Fables

When we consider the telling of the *Moral Fables*, we should consider the significance of the order in which they are told. This has caused some difficulty because, in the few surviving witnesses, there are many differences, so that the "correct" order, or even the existence of a correct order, may become a matter for conjecture, with the orders of Bannatyne and Bassandyne being most frequently discussed, because individuals have shown preferences for Bannatyne's or Bassandyne's readings within the poems.[1] Since the witnesses are removed by many years from Henryson's own time— there is no autograph manuscript—and they come from an era when a print might be the source of a manuscript, decisions cannot be made hastily.

Three manuscripts, the Bannatyne, Makculloch and Asloan, have some of the *Fables*, with that of Bannatyne offering the greatest number, ten of the thirteen, omitting only "The Fox, the Wolf, and the Cadger," "The Fox, the Wolf, and the Husbandman" and "The Wolf and the Wether." The Asloan MS now has only one fable, "The Two Mice," but the table of contents shows that it originally contained six others. The Makculloch MS gives only "The Prologue" and "The Cock and the Jasp" of the *Fables*, among a variety of poems copied in about 1500, "in another hand" on blank leaves among the lecture notes taken earlier by Magnus Makculloch, when he studied in Louvain. The Bassandyne Print of 1571 has all of the *Fables*, as have the Charteris Print (1569), the Harleian MS (1571), the Hart Print (1621) and the Smith Print (1577), using an order which has become known as traditional in editions of Henryson's *Poems*. These complete witnesses differ also in containing only Henryson's *Fables*, while the three incomplete witnesses have additional works, of Henryson and other authors, interpolated among the *Fables*. The only constant pattern to be found among the varying witnesses is the placing of "The Cock and the Jasp" after "The Prologue," and the sequence of the three fox fables: "The Cock and the Fox," "The Fox and the Wolf" and "The Trial of the Fox," for which there is internal evidence.[2]

---

[1] See Ch. I: 2, note 5.

[2] See Ch. I: 3, note 6. The Makculloch MS does not contain the fox fables; in the case of the Asloan MS, I refer to the table of contents.

The evidence of the Makculloch MS is rather too brief to allow us to draw more conclusions than that the writer of the later hand admired the opening section of Henryson's *Fables* and was presumably sensitive to the sequence implied in the conclusion of "The Prologue" and the beginning of "The Cock and the Jasp." We may note in passing that this glimpse of the *Fables* gives a reading of the lines in the opening stanza of "The Prologue" which may be the most vigorous and plausible of any of the variants describing the purpose of fables:

> and alss þe causs quhy þai ferst begane
> was to repreif þe of þi myslewyng
> of man be figowr of ane oþer thing.
>
> (Stevenson, 1918: 3, lines 5–7)[3]

The Asloan MS has a varied collection of works in prose and verse, compiled by the scribe John Asloan during the reign of James V. The list of contents shows that the manuscript originally contained some 70 items, but only 41 have survived. There are several references to Henryson in the table of contents, including one to a poem, now missing, "Dreme on fut by forth," of which no other trace can be found. Seven of the *Fables* are mentioned, with the last named now the only survivor among those selected, separated from its fellows by four other poems, as shown in the table:

Itm̄ þe fablis of Esope And first of the paddok and þe mouss xlij
Itm̄ þe preching of þe swallow .... xliij
Itm̄ þe lyoun and þe mouss .... xliiij
Itm̄ of chanticlere and þe fox xlv
Itm̄ of þe tod and þe wolf .... xlvj
Itm̄ þe parliament of bestis .... xlvij
Itm̄ By a palace as I couth pass .... xlviij
Itm̄ a ballat of treuth xlix
Itm̄ þe buke of þe howlat l
Itm̄ þe talis of þe fyve bestis .... lj
Itm̄ þe wplandis mouss & borowstovnis .... lij

(Craigie, 1923: xiv–xv)

Of these works, only the last three remain. Asloan is emphatic in placing "The Paddock and the Mouse" as the first of the *Fables*; but unfortunately his reasons are not explained in any surviving leaves of the manuscript.

A perusal of the contents shows that the manuscript has sections of works which are related by subject matter, but these are less distinctly

---

[3] See Ch. II: 8, note 1.

separated than the sections in the Bannatyne MS, and the divisions may have occurred simply as Asloan gained access to his sources rather than because he followed a scheme. The first items, for example, are in prose (with the exception of "The Book of Chess") and are generally theological or historical, beginning with the one described tartly by Craigie as "a long and dull treatise on Penance and Confession, in eleven chapters and extending to 80 pages" (Craigie, 1923: vi). The poems which follow are often related in style or content to their neighbours, as in the case of the six *Fables* and three "diuerss ballatis of our ladye," but an isolated fable and similar "ballatis" are scattered among the other poems. The divisions are largely unstated and, as already mentioned, less rigorous than those imposed by Bannatyne, who included his plan and introductory and concluding remarks in the addresses to his readers. Thus Asloan's table of contents is likely to be simply a record of the growth of a private collection gathered over a long period as sources became available.

Evidence for unity and integrity in the *Fables* in the Bassandyne Print and the other witnesses using this order may be found on structural and thematic grounds, but appears to be lacking if we look only at those of the *Fables* which are in the Bannatyne MS. We may miss a sense of unity because we are restricting our vision, and looking only at works which are interspersed within a section of the manuscript, when we should consider the collection as a whole.

The Bannatyne MS is a large collection (of 410 poems), planned and gathered over a number of years. It was probably intended for publication, although this would have been very unlikely in Scotland after the Reformation, when the publication of any bawdy and frivolous works was strongly discouraged. The whole manuscript reveals Bannatyne's taste and skill, and is arranged in five parts, covering a wide range of religious and secular poetry, set out in the first address—"The Wryttar to the Reidaris":

Now ʒe haif heir this ilk buik sa provydit
That in fyve pairtis It is dewly devydit
1 The first concernis god*is* gloir and ouir saluatioun
2 The nixt ar morale /grave And als besyd it
3 grund on gud counsale. The thrid I will not hyd it
Ar blyith and glaid Maid for ouir consollatioun.
4 The ferd of luve /and thair richt reformatioun.
5 The fyift ar tailis and storeis weill discydit
Reid as ʒe pleiss /I neid no moir narratioun.
(Ritchie, Vol. II, 1928: 1, lines 10–18)

The manuscript was finally assembled "in tyme of pest," in 1568, when Bannatyne and his family had to spend months in isolation to avoid infection, in the circumstances described in dramatic style by Sir Walter Scott, in his "Memoir of George Bannatyne," prepared for the members of the Bannatyne Club, and included as an appendix to Ritchie's edition of the manuscript:

> In this dreadful period, when hundreds, finding themselves sur-
> rounded by danger and death, renounced all care save that of
> selfish precautions for their safety, and all thoughts save ap-
> prehensions of infection, George Bannatyne had the courageous
> energy to form and execute the plan of saving the literature
> of a whole nation; and, undisturbed by the universal mourning
> for the dead, and general fears of the living, to devote himself
> to the task of collecting and recording the triumphs of human
> genius;—thus, amid the wreck of all that was mortal, employing
> himself in preserving the lays by which immortality is at once
> given to others, and obtained for the writer himself.
>
> (Ritchie, Vol. I, 1934: cxxix–cxxx)

We may find this praise extravagant, but it is balanced by Scott's estimate of Bannatyne's own poems which, although tactful, is quite unambiguous, and summarized by his remark that "the reader ... may probably be of the opinion that our Patron showed himself merciful in the sparing and moderate example which they afford of his poetical powers" (Ritchie, Vol. I, 1934: cxxxi). Since the Manuscript is such a rich source of poems and guide to sixteenth-century taste, perhaps no praise could be too generous.

The deliberate arrangement of the manuscript deals in an orderly way with Bannatyne's perception of life and literature. Ramson has summarized the five parts as follows:

> The first ... sought to communicate between man and God.
> The second counselled—it accepted the vastness of the differ-
> ence between God's knowledge and man's and advised man on
> how to cope best with his lot; the third and fourth developed
> man's understanding of this difference and the place of art in
> making it bearable ... The fifth ... section ... acknowledged
> the basic didactic function of poetry ... It was essentially moral
> and deeply Christian but marked by the tolerance only possible
> to someone comfortable in his faith.
>
> (Aitken/McDiarmid/Thomson, 1977: 180–181)

The summary suggests a unified and continuing plan, leading to the cli-mactic fifth section, with which we are most concerned. This section is more than a demonstration of poetry's didactic powers, since the poems offer an account of man's nature and place in creation, his duties and his shortcomings, an exposition which would be almost unbearable to anyone who was not "comfortable in his faith." In the terrifying circumstances of an outbreak of plague, the needs to repent and amend one's life, to avoid a disease thought to be God's punishment would be most urgent considerations, so that the section is an appropriate conclusion to an anthology which reflects the tastes and mores of its time and place.

We must beware of posthumous awards of intentions to poets and editors, but we find that Bannatyne has frankly stated some of his plans. His addresses, "The Wryttar to the Reidaris," which open and close the sections, show evidence of his editorial judgement and his intention to use it. The divisions are carefully arranged and ordered, and the fourth part is further subdivided, as announced:

> Heir followis ballatis of luve
> Devydit in four pairtis The first
> Ar songis of luve The secound ar
> Contemptis of luve And evill wemen
> The thrid ar contempis of evill
> fals vicius men And the fourt
> Ar ballatis detesting of luve
> And lichery   (Ritchie, Vol. III, 1928: 240)

Nothing about the planning of the task seems random, and we can feel confident that Bannatyne also exercised his own idiosyncratic judgement in the selection and ordering of the poems which appear in the fable section. We find, as well as the variations of a rapid and sometimes careless copier, alterations in the texts which were made deliberately and freely, for example the Protestant revisions in Henryson's *Fables*, which removed references considered too popish for post-Reformation taste and substituted lines less likely to give offence. An example may be found in the concluding stanza of "The Trial of the Fox," where the lines "O Mary myld medeato of mercy meke / Sitt doun before thy sone celestiall" have been altered to "O lord eternall medeator for ws mast meik / Sitt doun before thy fader celestiall" (Ritchie, Vol. IV, 1934: 181, lines 330–331). The emendations may be seen on the manuscript.[4]

Bannatyne was an uninhibited editor, and, although he follows the accepted sequences of the fox fables and "The Prologue" and "The Cock and the Jasp," we should not be surprised to find that in other places he diverges sharply from traditional orders and interpolates other works in an anthology which is of his own selection. We should look instead at the final

---

[4] Alasdair MacDonald refers to this and similar examples of Bannatyne's revisions (MacDonald, 1983: 416–420).

arrangement of the fifth part, to see how neighbouring poems sit with one another, and how the editor moves from the fanciful, timeless world of fable to his own historical era. In considering these specific rather than general intentions, we must at times be somewhat speculative in some of our assumptions of Bannatyne's exact intentions when he arranged the fifth part, as shown in Table 2 (Ch. I: 4).

Bannatyne's own words set the tone, when he announces

> thair ar hid but dowt
> Grave materis wyiss and sapient
> Vnder the workis of poyetis gent.
>
> (Ritchie, Vol. IV, 1934: 116–117, lines 4–6)

"The Preaching of the Swallow," with its cosmic picture of creation and man's place in it, makes an excellent opening piece, since it tells of the unheeded warnings given to wayward man and the punishment which attends his wilfulness, a sobering beginning to the section. It is followed by another fable of birds, Holland's "Buke of the Howlat." There is a superficial resemblance to the preceding poem, in the presence of a narrator who journeys into the countryside and overhears the conversation of birds, and a deeper one in its final stress on the inevitability of the working of the created universe. The owl cannot alter his nature and unhappy place in creation, just as the swallow cannot affect the attitudes and fate of the birds who ignore her warning. Although the system of offices and speeches of the birds in "The Buke of the Howlat" offer a more elaborate and sophisticated parody of human life, the message to man is very similar.

These poems are followed by the early group of Henryson's fox fables: "The Cock and the Fox," "The Fox and the Wolf" and "The Trial of the Fox." They take place in a fabulous but fairly just world, where, even if victims are not always saved, known villains are harshly punished for their misdeeds. Harsh judgement is a factor common to the next work, Henryson's "Orpheus and Eurydice," which ends with a lengthy *moralitas* stressing one of Henryson's most important themes—the separation of the soul and the body. In the references to the soul's upward aspirations, always marred by the body's downward tendencies, illustrated by thoughts of the soul's blindness, its bondage in the body and images of wheels (Fortune's and Ixion's) there are suggestions of the prologue to "The Preaching of the Swallow" and the *moralitas* of "The Paddock and the Mouse." "Orpheus and Eurydice" precedes another allegory which draws its message from human and spiritual worlds rather than that of the fabulous animal characters. This is "The Bludy Serk," Henryson's version of the favourite medieval allegory of Christ, the lover-knight.

Bannatyne now moves to his largest group of Henryson's *Fables*, beginning with the opening sequence in the traditional order, "The Prologue" and "The Cock and the Jasp," but following this with the fable which has the last place in complete witnesses—"The Paddock and the Mouse." We must assume that an editor of Bannatyne's taste and care would not miss the implication of the lines he copied at the end of "The Prologue":

And to begyn first at a cok he wrate
Seikand his meit quhilk fand a goly stone
Off quhome þe fable ȝe sall heir annone
(Ritchie, Vol. IV: 208, lines 61-63)

which suggest the beginning of a series. Similarly, he would not overlook the sense of finality in the last stanza of the *moralitas* of "The Paddock and the Mouse":

Adew my freind and gife þat ony speiris
of this fable so schortly I conclude
Thow say I left the laif vnto þe freiris
To mak a sample or similitud
Now chryst for ws þat deit on the rud
of saule and lyf as thow art saluiour
grant ws to pass in till a blissit hour.
(Ritchie, Vol. IV, 1934: 217, lines 193-199)

I have suggested elsewhere that the *moralitates* of these fables could sum up the lessons which Henryson wants to leave with his audience, but perfect understanding is not to be assumed in erring man, and such a brief summary would be incomplete and inadequate. The fables which follow have some of the most accessible of the *moralitates*, clearly expressed in the words of the Narrator, the sheep and Aesop. There seems no need for explanation from the friars. After "The Paddock and the Mouse" comes "The Two Mice," with a lighthearted tale of a similar protagonist and a *moralitas* which has resemblances in form and content. We should probably not see this as a way of restating the moral theme, but rather as an attempt to show that there can be contentment in the simple life, as well as a struggle from which death must be the release.

The two sheep fables, "The Sheep and the Dog" and "The Wolf and the Lamb," make a sad pair, illustrating increases of scale in the contrasts between the protagonists, the injustices dealt to the weaker beasts and in the pessimistic conclusions to be drawn. Truth and justice are progressively more strongly assailed and eventually overwhelmed by falsehood and abuse of power in their most cruel form, so that the two fables can logically be placed together to emphasize this development. We can be glad to find in "The Lion and the Mouse" a tiny heroine with slight physical strength and lively intellect who gains a just hearing. This comforting fable, with its happy ending and prompt earthly rewards, is the last selected by Bannatyne, whereas in the traditional orders it is the central fable, which concludes the earlier and more optimistic section.

At this point Bannatyne's selection turns away from Aesop's animal world to the dazzling scenes described by Dunbar in "The Thrissil and the Rois" and "The Goldyn Targe." Although the first of these refers to the court of the lion, the spectacle is remote and unearthly, unlike the land-scape of "The Lion and the Mouse," where Henryson's aureate descriptions enhance the beauty of familiar scenes. There is a sharp contrast in the work which follows, "The Three Friars of Berwick," a jolting *fabliau* which is an entertaining corrective to any thought that human life and love could long exist on the rarefied plane of "The Goldyn Targe." This poem has been doubtfully attributed to Dunbar, but not by Bannatyne. Dunbar's "Tretis of the Twa Mariit Wemen and the Wedo" shows his ability to write of love with devastating cynicism, but the barbs of "The Three Friars of Berwick" are blunter. Friars, faithless wives and imperceptive husbands were, after all, fair game, and many poets aimed at them, but few works had the stinging accuracy of "The Twa Mariit Wemen and the Wedo."

There is a similar reversal in the next pair of poems. "Cockelbie Sow" is a rambling, fantastic variation on the theme of the talents, with wild adventures and happy endings, hilariously far from real life in its exaggerated illustrations of sound advice. "Robene and Makyne," Henryson's elegantly concise *pastourelle*, gives bitter and accurate comment on life and love. Both poems commend the use of opportunity, but in immeasurably different ways. Again, the latter poem offers a sharply realistic corrective to the former's fantasy, and the effect is like that of the surprising reversals found in Henryson's *Fables*. If such lessons are intended, they suggest a character for Bannatyne which is more cynical, and somewhat more interesting, than Scott's idealistic picture.

The fifth part of the manuscript concludes with Bellenden's "Second Proheme of the History of the Chronicles of Scotland," bringing the reader to Bannatyne's own times. It is written in a stylized fashion, with many mythological references, but in the accepted style of historical poetry of its era, taking the collection to the current versions of the courtly scenes which have been described throughout the fable section. The reader has been returned to Bannatyne's present and has received a good deal of guidance during the journey: to accept his fate, lead a godly and repentant life and seize his opportunities are only some of the lessons. We may remember Bannatyne's circumstances and consider that he seems to have followed this advice. He had to endure the threat of plague and remain in seclusion to escape God's vengeance, and he used his enforced isolation to arrange and preserve the literature he found most precious. We may rely on the clear messages he sends from "The Wryttar to the Redar," and value his orderly scheme and editorial taste. The clear perception of man's nature and the encouragement to amend life confirm Ramson's estimate of the fifth part as "essentially moral and deeply Christian but marked by the tolerance only possible to someone comfortable in his faith."

We may wonder about those of Henryson's *Fables* which do not appear in the manuscript: "The Fox, the Wolf and the Cadger," "The Fox, the Wolf, and the Husbandman" and "The Wolf and the Wether." It may be that Bannatyne had no source for them, if the *Fables* were published or circulated in small groups at intervals, as suggested by Lyall (1985: 17). It is not necessary, however, to assume this, and it need not suggest a lack of unity in the *Fables*, in any case, since works which are part of an overall plan need not be written in sequence; we may think, for example, of Shakespeare's history plays. It is also probable that the omissions were quite deliberate, and made because Bannatyne found no need for those *Fables* in his own scheme of arrangement for the diverse collection in his manuscript. He may have been satisfied that warnings against covetousness were given more lightheartedly in "Cockelbie Sow" and against false appearances in "The Buke of the Howlat," and examples of deception abound in "The Three Friars of Berwick." Another editor might question the inclusion of "Robene and Makyne" with the fables rather than the love poems, or think that "The Bludy Serk" should be placed with the religious works. The writer of the later hand who has added titles to the poems has classified only the works from "The Preaching of the Swallow" to "The Goldyn Targe" as fables. Finally we must conclude that Bannatyne's arrangement reveals his own views and priorities in his choice and ordering of poems.

What may we eventually discover about the Bannatyne manuscript? Only that an editor of considerable taste and independent attitude, with an urgent desire to preserve the literature of Scotland, compiled a manuscript in the way which seemed best to him. Should we then expect anything but an idiosyncratic arrangement? Although Bassandyne's Print and the witnesses which follow it show us evidence for structural and thematic unity within the *Fables*, we should not look for such features within some of the works in part of the manuscript but rather in the collection as a whole, demonstrated by Bannatyne's adherence to his scheme. Thus we should regard those of the *Fables* which appear simply as a part of Bannatyne's selection of Scottish literature. We may assume that he imposed his own order, overriding other considerations, whether perceived or unnoticed. The manuscript deserves consideration for its own sake, as a store of poetry of many kinds and a source for much more than Henryson's *Fables*.

Bibliography

Aitken, A.J., ed. *Lowland Scots.* Edinburgh: Association for Scottish Literary Studies, 1973. ASLS Occasional Papers, No. 2.

Aitken, A.J., M.P. McDiarmid and D.S. Thomson, eds. *Bards and Makars. Scottish Language and Literature: Medieval and Renaissance.* Glasgow: U of Glasgow, 1977.

Baldwin, Charles Sears. *Medieval Rhetoric and Poetic (to 1400): Interpreted from Representative Works.* New York: Macmillan, 1928.

Baltzell, Jane. "Rhetorical 'Amplification' and 'Abbreviation' and the Structure of Medieval Narrative." *PCP* 2 (1967): 32–39.

Bastin, Julia. *Recueil général des Isopets.* Vol. 2. Paris: Societé des Anciens Textes Français, 1930.

Bauman, R. "The Folk Tale and Oral Tradition in the Fables of Henryson." *Fabula* 6 (1963): 108–124.

Benson, L.D., ed. *The Learned and the Lewed: Studies in Chaucer and Medieval Literature.* Cambridge, MA: Harvard UP, 1974. Harvard English Studies 5.

Bethurum, Dorothy. "Chaucer's Point of View as Narrator in the Love Lyrics." *PMLA* 74.4 (1959): 511–520.

——, ed. *Critical approaches to Medieval Literature: Selected Papers from the English Institute, 1958–59.* New York: Columbia UP, 1960.

Blake, N.F., ed. *The History of Reynard the Fox. Translated from the Dutch Original by William Caxton.* London: Oxford UP, 1970. EETS 263.

Blanchot, Jean-Jacques and Claude Graf, eds. *Actes du 2ᵉ Colloque de Langue et de Litterature Ecossaises (Moyen Age et Renaissance). Université de Strasbourg 5–11 juillet 1978.* Strasbourg: Université de Strasbourg, 1978.

Bloom, Edward. "The Allegorical Principle." *ELH* 18.3 (1951): 163–190.

Booth, Wayne C. *The Rhetoric of Fiction.* Chicago: U of Chicago P, 1961.

——. *A Rhetoric of Irony*. Chicago: U of Chicago P, 1974.

Brewer, D.S. *Symbolic Stories: Traditional Narratives of the Family Drama in English Literature*. Bury St. Edmunds: D.S. Brewer, Rowan and Littlefield, 1960.

——. *Traditional Stories and their Meanings*. London: The English Association, 1983. The English Association Presidential Address, 1983.

——, ed. *Chaucer and Chaucerians: Critical Studies in Middle English Literature*. London: Nelson, 1966.

——, ed. *Geoffrey Chaucer*. London: Bell, 1974. Writers and Their Background.

Brown, Carleton, ed. *English Lyrics of the XIIIth Century*. Oxford: Clarendon, 1971; first published 1932.

Brown, Jennifer, ed. *Scottish Society in the Fifteenth Century*. London: Arnold, 1977.

Butler, Christopher. *Number Symbolism*. Ideas and Forms in English Literature, gen. ed. John Lawlor. London: Routledge and Kegan Paul, 1970.

Burrow, John A. "Henryson: *The Preiching of the Swallow*." *EIC* 25.1 (1975): 25–37.

Campbell, Alexander. *An Introduction to the History of Poetry in Scotland, from the Beginning of the Thirteenth Century down to the Present Time*. New York: Garland Publishing, 1972. Facsimile of a copy in the Harvard U Library, 10457.4*, first published 1798.

Carens, Marilyn Mumford. "A Prolegomenon for the Study of Robert Henryson." Diss. Pennsylvania State U, 1974.

Clark, George. "Henryson and Aesop: The Fable Transformed." *ELH* 43.1 (1976): 1–18.

Craigie, W.A., ed. *The Asloan Manuscript: A Miscellany in Prose and Verse. Written by John Asloan in the Reign of James the Fifth*. Vol. I. Edinburgh and London: Blackwood, 1923. STS n.s. 14.

Crosby, Ruth. "Oral Delivery in the Middle Ages." *Speculum* 11.1 (1936): 88–110.

———. "Chaucer and the Custom of Oral Delivery." *Speculum* 13.4 (1938): 413–432.

Crowne, D.K. "A Date for the Composition of Henryson's Fables." *JEGP* 61.3 (1962): 583–590.

Cruttwell, Patrick. "Makers and Persons." *Hudson Review* 12.4 (1959–60): 457–507.

———. "Two Scots Poets: Dunbar and Henryson." In *The Age of Chaucer*, ed. B. Ford, Harmondsworth: Penguin, 1954, Vol. I of *The Pelican Guide to English Literature*. 175–187.

Curtius, E.R. *European Literature and the Latin Middle Ages*. Trans. W.R. Trask. London: Routledge and Kegan Paul, 1953. Originally published as *Europäische Literatur und Lateinisches Mittelalter*, Bern, 1948.

Daalder, Joost, ed. *Sir Thomas Wyatt: Collected Poems*. London: Oxford UP, 1975.

Dahlberg, Charles. "Chaucer's Cock and Fox." *JEGP* 53.3 (1954): 277–290.

Datta, Kitty Scoular. "New Light on Marvell's 'A Dialogue between the Soul and Body'." *RenQ* 22.3 (1969): 242–255.

Daugherty, Evelyn Newlyn (see also Newlyn, Evelyn). "The 'Kyrnall' and the 'Nuttis Schell': The Poetry of Robert Henryson." Diss. Syracuse U, 1977.

De Maria, Robert, Jr. "The Ideal Reader: A Critical Fiction." *PMLA* 93.3 (1978): 463–474.

Donaldson, E. Talbot. *Speaking of Chaucer*. London: The Athlone Press, 1970.

Donovan, Mortimer J. "The *Moralite* of the Nun's Priest's Sermon." *JEGP* 52.4 (1953): 498–508.

Eco, Umberto. *The Role of the Reader: Explorations in the Semiotics of Texts*. Bloomington, IN: Indiana UP, 1984.

Ellenberger, B. *The Latin Element in the Vocabulary of the Earliest Makars, Henryson and Dunbar*. Lund: Gleerup, 1977. Lund Studies in English 51.

Elliot, Charles, ed. *Robert Henryson: Poems.* 2nd ed. Oxford: Clarendon, 1974; first published 1963. Clarendon Medieval and Tudor Series.

Elliot, Robert C. *The Literary Persona.* Chicago and London: U of Chicago P, 1982.

Ellwood Smith, M. "The Fable as Poetry in English Criticism." *MLN* 32.8 (1917): 466–470

Falke, Anne. "The Comic Functions of the Narrator in *Troilus and Criseyde.*" *Neophil* 68.1 (1984): 134–141.

Fletcher, Angus. *Allegory: The Theory of a Symbolic Mode.* Ithaca, NY: Cornell UP, 1964.

Fletcher, John. *Novel and Reader.* London and Boston: Marion Boyars, 1980.

Foucault, Michel. "What is an Author?" *The Foucault Reader.* Ed. Paul Rabinov. Harmondsworth: Penguin, 1991. 101–120. Tr. Josué V. Harari. First published in *Textual Strategies: Perspectives in Post-Structuralist Criticism*, ed. J. Harari. London: Methuen, 1980. 141–160.

Fowler, Alistair. *Spenser and the Numbers of Time.* London: Routledge and Kegan Paul, 1964.

——, ed. *Silent Poetry: Essays in Numerological Analysis.* London: Routledge and Kegan Paul, 1970.

Fox, Denton. "Henryson's Fables." *ELH* 29.4 (1962): 337–356.

——. "Henryson and Caxton." *JEGP* 67.4 (1968): 586–593.

——. "A Scoto-Danish Stanza, Wyatt, Henryson and the Two Mice." *N&Q* n.s. 18.6 (1971): 203–207.

——, ed. *The Poems of Robert Henryson.* Oxford: Clarendon, 1981.

——, and William A. Ringler. Introduction. *The Bannatyne Manuscript.* National Library of Scotland Adv. MS 1. 1. 6. London: Scolar, in association with The National Library of Scotland, 1980.

Frank, R.W. " "The Art of Reading Medieval Personification Allegory." *ELH* 20.4 (1953): 237–250.

Fratus, David Joseph. "Robert Henryson's *Moral Fables*: Tradition, Text, and Translation." Diss. U of Iowa, 1971.

Frese, Dolores Warwick. "The *Nun's Priest's Tale*: Chaucer's Identified Master Piece?" *ChauR* 16.4 (1982): 330–343.

Freud, Sigmund. *Beyond the Pleasure Principle*. Vol. XVIII of *The Standard Edition of the Complete Psychological Works of Sigmund Freud*. Gen. ed. and trans. James Strachey. London: Hogarth and the Institute of Psycho-Analysis, 1968; first published 1955.

Friedman, John Block. "Henryson, the Friars and the *Confessio Reynardi*." *JEGP* 66.4 (1967): 550–561.

Gabbard, Gregory Norman. "The Animal-Human Double Context in the Beast Fables and Beast Tales of Chaucer and Henryson." Diss. U of Texas at Austin, 1968.

Gallo, Ernest. *The Poetria Nova and its Sources in Early Rhetorical Doctrine*. The Hague and Paris: Mouton, 1971. De Proprietatibus Litterarum edenda curat C. H. van Schooneveld, Indiana U Series Maior, 10.

Geoffrey of Vinsauf. *Documentum de Modo et Arte Dictandi et Versificandi. (Instruction in the Method and Art of Speaking and Versifying)*. Trans. Roger P. Parr. Milwaukee, WI: Marquette UP, 1968.

Gerke, Robert S. "Studies in the Tradition and Morality of Henryson's Fables." Diss. U of Notre Dame, 1968.

Godschalk, Anne M. "Robert Henryson's *Moral Fables*: Metaphor and Moral View." Diss. U of Cincinatti, 1973.

Gray, Douglas. *Robert Henryson*. Leiden: E.J. Brill, 1979. Medieval and Renaissance Authors Series, gen. eds. John Norton-Smith and Douglas Gray.

Greenblatt, Stephen J., ed. *Allegory and Representation. Selected Papers from the English Institute, 1979–80*. n.s. 5. Baltimore and London: Johns Hopkins UP, 1981.

Handford, S.A., trans. *Fables of Aesop*. Harmondsworth: Penguin, 1979; first published 1954.

Hardy, Barbara. *Tellers and Listeners. The Narrative Imagination*. London: U of London, The Athlone Press, 1975.

Harrington, David V. "Chaucer's Man of Law's Tale: Rhetoric and Emotion." *MSpr* 61.4 (1967): 353–362.

Heidtmann, P. "A Bibliography of Henryson, Dunbar, and Douglas, 1912–1968." *ChauR* 5.1 (1970): 75–82.

Heiserman, Arthur R. *The Novel before the Novel: Essays and Discussion about the Beginnings of Prose Fiction in the West.* Chicago: U of Chicago P, 1977.

Henderson, Arnold C. "'Of Heigh or Lough Estat': Medieval Fabulists as Social Critics." *Viator* 9 (1978): 265–290.

——. "Medieval Beasts and Modern Cages: The Making of Meaning in Fables and Bestiaries." *PMLA* 97.1 (1982): 40–49.

Holland, Norman N. *The Dynamics of Literary Response.* New York: Oxford UP, 1968.

Honig, Edwin. *Dark Conceit: The Making of Allegory.* Evanston: Northwestern UP, 1959.

Hopper, Vincent F. *Medieval Number Symbolism: Its Sources, Meaning, and Influence on Thought and Expression.* New York: Cooper Square, 1969; first published 1938. Columbia U Studies in English and Comparative Literature 132.

Huizinga, J. *The Waning of the Middle Ages.* Trans. F. Hopman. Harmondsworth: Penguin, 1979; first published 1924.

Jack, R.D.S. " "Caxton's *Mirrour of the World* and Henryson's 'Taill of the Cok and the Jasp'." *ChauR* 13.2 (1978): 157–165.

Jacobs, Joseph. *The Fables of Aesop.* London: Macmillan, 1979; first published 1894. Macmillan Facsimile Classics Series.

Jamieson, I.W.A. "The Poetry of Robert Henryson: A Study of the Use of Source Material." Diss. U of Edinburgh, 1964.

——. "Henryson's 'Fabillis': an Essay towards a Revaluation." *Words, Waite-Atu Studies in English* 2 (1966): 20–31.

——. "A Further Source for Henryson's 'Fabillis'." *N&Q* n.s. 14.11 (1967): 403–405.

——. "Henryson's *Taill of the Wolf and the Wedder.*" *SSL* 6.4 (1969): 248–257.

——. "The Minor Poems of Robert Henryson." *SSL* 9.2–3 (1971–2): 125–147.

——. "The Beast Tale in Middle Scots." *Parergon* 2 (1972): 26–36.

——. " 'To Preue Thare Preching be a Poesye': Some Thoughts on Henryson's Poetics." *Parergon* 8 (1974): 24–36.

——. "Some Attitudes to Poetry in Late Fifteenth-Century Scotland." *SSL* 15 (1980): 28–42.

Jenkins, Anthony White. "The Mind and Art of Robert Henryson." Diss. U of California, Berkeley, 1968.

——. "Henryson's *The Fox, the Wolf and the Cadger* Again." *SSL* 4. (1967): 107–112.

Kawin, Bruce F. *Telling It Again and Again: Repetition in Literature and Film*. Ithaca and London: Cornell UP, 1972.

Kermode, Frank. *The Sense of an Ending. Studies in the Theory of Fiction*. New York: Oxford UP, 1967. The Mary Flexner Lectures, 1967.

——. *Novel and Narrative*. Glasgow: U of Glasgow, 1972. The twenty-fourth W.P. Ker Memorial Lecture, delivered in the U of Glasgow, 9th March, 1972.

——. *The Genesis of Secrecy. On the Interpretation of Narrative*. Cambridge, MA: Harvard UP, 1979.

——. "Secrets and Narrative Sequence." *CritI* 7.1 (1980): 83–101.

Khinoy, Stephan. "Tale-Moral Relationships in Henryson's *Moral Fables*." *SSL* 17 (1982): 99–115.

Kindrick, Robert L. "Lion or Cat? Henryson's Characterization of James III." *SSL* 14 (1979): 123–135.

——. *Robert Henryson*. Boston: Twayne, 1979. Twayne's English Authors Series, TEAS 274, ed. George D. Economou.

——. "Politics and Poetry in the Court of James III." *SSL* 19 (1984): 40–55.

Kinghorn, A.M. "The Medieval Makars." *TSLL* 1.1 (1959): 73–88.

——. "The Minor Poems of Robert Henryson." *SSL* 3.1 (1965): 30–40.

——, ed. *The Middle Scots Poets*. London: Arnold, 1970. York Medieval Texts.

114

Kinsley, James. "Robert Henryson." *TLS* 14 Nov. 1952: 743.

——, ed. *Scottish Poetry: A Critical Survey*. London: Cassell, 1955.

——, ed. *The Poems of William Dunbar*. Oxford: Clarendon, 1979.

Koban, Charles. "Hearing Chaucer Out: The Art of Persuasion in the *Wife of Bath's Tale*." *ChauR* 5.3 (1970): 225–239.

Koonce, B.G. "Satan the Fowler." *MS* 21 (1959): 176–184.

Kratzmann, Gregory. *Anglo-Scottish Literary Relations 1430–1550*. Cambridge: Cambridge UP, 1980.

——. "Henryson's *Fables*: 'the Subtell Dyte of Poetry'." *SSL* 20 (1985): 49–70.

Lall, Rama Rani. *Satiric Fable in English: A Critical Study of the Animal Tales of Chaucer, Spenser, Dryden and Orwell*. New Delhi: New Statesman, 1979.

Levy, H.L. "As Myn Auctour Seyth." *MÆ* 12 (1943): 25–39.

Lindsay, Maurice. *History of Scottish Literature*. London: Robert Hale, 1977.

Lyall, Roderick J. "Politics and Poetry in Fifteenth and Sixteenth Century Scotland." *SLJ* 3.2 (1976): 5–29.

——. "Henryson and Boccaccio: A Problem in the Study of Sources." *Anglia* 99.1–2 (1981): 38–59.

——. "The Development of Henryson's *Morall Fabillis* from Their Sources." Unpublished paper, 1985.

MacCracken, Henry Noble, ed. *The Minor Poems of John Lydgate*. Part II, Secular Poems. London: Humphrey Milford, 1934. EETS 192.

McDiarmid, Matthew. "Robert Henryson in His Poems." Aitken /McDiarmid/Thomson, 1977. 27–40.

MacDonald, Alasdair A. "Poetry, Politics, and Reformation Censorship in Sixteenth-Century Scotland." *ES* 64.5 (1983): 410–421.

McDonald, Craig. "The Perversion of Law in Robert Henryson's Fable of the *Fox, the Wolf and the Husbandman*." *MÆ* 49.2 (1980): 244–253.

MacDonald, D. "Narrative Art in Henryson's Fables." *SSL* 3.2 (1965): 101–113.

———. "Henryson and Chaucer: Cock and Fox." *TSLL* 8.4 (1967): 451–461.

———. "Chaucer's Influence on Henryson's Fables: The Use of Proverbs and Sententiae." *MÆ* 39.1 (1970): 21–27.

Mackenzie, W. Mackay, ed. *The Poems of William Dunbar.* London: Faber, 1960; first published 1932.

MacQueen, John. "The Text of Henryson's *Morall Fabillis.*" *Innes Rev* 14 (1963): 3–9.

———. *Robert Henryson: A Study of the Major Narrative Poems.* Oxford: Clarendon, 1967.

———. *Allegory.* London: Methuen, 1970. The Critical Idiom, gen. ed. John D. Jump, 14.

Manning, Stephen. "The Nun's Priest's Morality, and the Medieval Attitude toward Fables." *JEGP* 59.3 (1960): 403–416.

Margoliouth, H.M., ed. *The Poems and Letters of Andrew Marvell.* Vol. I, Poems. Oxford: Clarendon, 1927.

Metcalfe, W.M., ed. *The Poems of Robert Henryson.* Paisley: Alexander Gardner, 1917.

Muecke, D.C. *The Compass of Irony.* London: Methuen, 1969.

———. *Irony.* London: Methuen, 1970. The Critical Idiom, gen. ed. John D. Jump, 13.

Muir, Edward. *Essays on Literature and Society.* London: Hogarth Press, rev. 1965; first published Philadelphia, 1949.

Murphy, James J. *Rhetoric in the Middle Ages. A History of Rhetorical Theory from Saint Augustine to the Renaissance.* Berkeley: U of California P, 1974.

———, ed. *Three Medieval Rhetorical Arts.* Berkeley: U of California P, 1971.

———, ed. *Medieval Eloquence: Studies in the Theory and Practice of Medieval Rhetoric.* Berkeley: U of California P, 1978.

Murtaugh, D.N. "Henryson's Animals." *TSLL* 14.3 (1972): 404–421.

Nelson, William. *Fact or Fiction. The Dilemma of the Renaissance Story-teller*. Cambridge, MA: Harvard UP, 1973.

Newlyn, Evelyn S. " "Robert Henryson and the Popular Fable Tradition in the Middle Ages." *JPC* 14.1 (1980): 108–118.

——. "Affective Style in Middle Scots: The Education of the Reader in Three Fables of Robert Henryson." *NMS* 26 (1982): 44–56.

Olson, Glending. "The Medieval Theory of Literature for Refreshment and its Use in the Fabliau Tradition." *SP* 71.3 (1974): 219–313.

Ong, Walter J. "The Writer's Audience is Always a Fiction." *PMLA* 90.1 (1975): 9–21.

Owst, G.R. *Literature and Pulpit in Medieval England*. Oxford: Basil Blackwell, 1961; first published 1933.

Patch, Howard R. *The Goddess Fortuna in Medieval Literature*. London: Frank Cass, 1967; first published 1927.

Pearsall, Derek. *John Lydgate*. London: Routledge and Kegan Paul, 1970.

Pope, Robert. "A Sly Toad, Physiognomy and the Problem of Deceit: Henryson's *The Paddok and the Mous*." *Neophil* 63.3 (1979): 461–468.

——. "Henryson's *The Sheep and Dog*." *EIC* 30.3 (1980): 205–214.

Regis, Edward, Jr. "Literature *by* the Reader: The 'Affective' Theory of Stanley Fish." *CE* 38.3 (1976): 263–280.

Reiss, Edmund. *William Dunbar*. Boston: Twayne, 1979.

——. "Chaucer and his Audience." *ChauR* 14.4 (1980): 390–402.

Ridley, F.H. "A Check List, 1956–1968, for Study of *The Kingis Quair*, the Poetry of Robert Henryson, Gawin Douglas, and William Dunbar." *SSL* 8.1 (1970): 30–51.

Ritchie, W. Tod, ed. *The Bannatyne Manuscript*. Edinburgh and London: Blackwood. Vol. I, 1934, STS 3rd series 5; Vol. II, 1928, STS n.s. 22; Vol. III, 1928, STS n.s. 23; Vol. IV, 1934. STS n.s. 26.

Roerecke, H.H. "The Integrity and Symmetry of Robert Henryson's *Moral Fables*." Diss. Pennsylvania State U, 1969.

Rollinson, Philip. *Classical Theories of Allegory and Christian Culture*. Pittsburgh: Duquesne UP, 1981. Duquesne Studies, Language and Literature Series, Vol. 3.

Rosenblatt, Louise M. *The Reader, the Text, the Poem. The Transactional Theory of the Literary Work*. Carbondale and Edwardsville: Southern Illinois UP, 1978.

Ross, Ian Simpson. *William Dunbar*. Leiden: Brill, 1981. Medieval and Renaissance Authors Series.

Rowland, Beryl. *Animals with Human Faces*. Knoxville: U of Tennessee P, 1972.

—, ed. *Chaucer and Middle English Studies in Honour of Rossell Hope Robbins*. London: Unwin, 1974.

Rowlands, Mary E. "The Fables of Robert Henryson." *DalR* 39 (1960): 491–502.

—. "Robert Henryson and the Scottish Courts of Law." *AUR* 39.127 (1961–2): 119–226.

Sands, Donald B., ed. *The History of Reynard the Fox. Translated and Printed by William Caxton in 1481*. Cambridge, MA: Harvard UP, 1960.

Scheps, Walter. "Chaucer's Anti-Fable: *Reductio Ad Absurdum* in the *Nun's Priest's Tale*." *LSE*, n.s. 4 (1970): 1–10.

Schoeck, Richard and Jerome Taylor, eds. *Chaucer Criticism*. Notre Dame, IN: U of Notre Dame P; Vol. I, 1960; Vol. II, 1961.

Scholes, Robert. *The Fabulators*. New York: Oxford UP, 1967; first published 1963.

—, ed. *Approaches to the Novel: Material for a Poetics*. Rev. ed. San Francisco: Chandler, 1966; first published 1961.

— and Robert Kellogg. *The Nature of Narrative*. New York: Oxford UP, 1966.

— and Carl H. Klaus, eds. *Elements of the Essay*. New York: Oxford UP, 1969.

Schrader, Richard J. "Some Backgrounds of Henryson." *SSL* 15 (1980): 124–138.

Scott, Tom, ed. *Late Medieval Scots Poetry. A Selection from the Makars and their Heirs down to 1610*. London: Heinemann, 1967.

Shallers, A. Paul. "The 'Nun's Priest's Tale': An Ironic Exemplum." *ELH* 42.3 (1975): 319–337.

Shire, Helena. *Song, Dance and Poetry of the Court of Scotland under King James VI*. Cambridge: Cambridge UP, 1969.

Siegel, Marsha. "Robert Henryson's Quest for a Morality." Diss. U of California, Berkeley, 1977.

Smalley, Beryl. *The Study of the Bible in the Middle Ages*. Oxford: Clarendon 1941.

——, ed. *Trends in Medieval Political Thought*. Oxford: Basil Blackwell, 1965.

Smith, George Gregory. *Scottish Literature: Character and Influence*. London: Macmillan, 1919.

——, ed. *The Poems of Robert Henryson*. Edinburgh and London: Blackwood; Vol. I, 1914; Vol. II, 1906; Vol. III, 1908. STS 55–58.

Sonning, Lee A. *A Handbook to Sixteenth Century Rhetoric*. London: Routledge and Kegan Paul, 1968.

Spanier, Sandra Whipple. "Structural Symmetry in Henryson's 'The Preiching of the Swallow'." *Comitatus* 10 (1979–80): 123–127.

Spearing, A.C. *Criticism and Medieval Poetry*. 2nd ed. London: Edward Arnold, 1972; first published 1964.

——. *Medieval Dream Poetry*. Cambridge: Cambridge UP, 1976.

——. "Central and Displaced Sovereignty in Three Medieval Poems." *RES* n.s. 33.131 (1982): 247–261.

Speirs, John. *The Scots Literary Tradition*. 2nd ed. London: Faber, 1962; first published Chatto and Windus, 1940.

Spitzer, Leo. "Note on the Poetic and Empirical 'I' in Medieval Authors." *Traditio* 4 (1946): 414–422.

Steegmuller, Francis, ed. and trans. *The Letters of Gustave Flaubert 1830–1857*. Cambridge, MA and London: Belknap Press of Harvard UP, 1980.

Steinley, Gary. "Introductory Remarks on Narratology." *CE* 38.3 (1976): 311–315.

Stevenson, George, ed. *Pieces from the Makculloch and the Gray MSS. Together with the Chepman and Myllar Prints.* Edinburgh and London: Blackwood, 1918. STS 1st series 65.

Suleiman, Susan R. and Inge Crosman. *The Reader in the Text.* Princeton: Princeton UP, 1980.

Sutton, Robert Francis. "The Moral Fables of Robert Henryson, the Scots Makar." Diss. U of Massachusetts, 1975.

Tolliver, H.E. "Robert Henryson: From *Moralitas* to Irony." *ES* 46.4 (1965): 300–309.

Tompkins, Jane P., ed. *Reader-Response Criticism: From Formalism to Post-Structuralism.* Baltimore and London: Johns Hopkins UP, 1980.

Trimpi, Wesley. "The Ancient Hypothesis of Fiction: An Essay on the origins of Literary Theory." *Traditio* 27 (1971): 1–79.

——. "The Quality of Fiction: The Rhetorical Transmission of Literary Theory." *Traditio* 30 (1974): 1–118.

Tuve, Rosemond. *Allegorical Imagery: Some Medieval Books and their Posterity.* Princeton: Princeton UP, 1966.

Van Buuren-Veenenbos, C.C. "John Asloan, an Edinburgh Scribe." *ES* 47.5 (1966): 365–372.

Varnhagen, Hermann. "Zu Mittelenglischen Gedichten." *Anglia* 2 (1879, reprinted 1963): 225–255.

Varty, Kenneth. *Reynard the Fox: A Study of the Fox in Medieval English Art.* Leicester: Leicester UP, 1967.

——. "The Pursuit of Reynard in Mediaeval English Literature and Art." *NMS* 8 (1964): 62–81.

Vickers, B. *Classical Rhetoric in English Poetry.* London: Macmillan, 1970.

Von Kreisler, Nicholas. "Henryson's Visionary Fable: Tradition and Craftsmanship in 'The Lyoun and the Mous'." *TSLL* 15.3 (1973): 391–403.

120

Waswo, Richard. "The Narrator of *Troilus and Criseyde.*" *ELH* 50.1 (1983): 1–25.

White, Hayden. "The Value of Narrativity in the Representation of Reality." *CritI* 7.1 (1980): 5–28.

Whiting, Bartlett Jere. *Proverbs, Sentences, and Proverbial Phrases from English Writings mainly before 1500*. Cambridge, MA: Harvard UP, 1968.

Wilson, George. "Chaucer and Oral Readings." *SAQ* 25.3 (1926): 283–299.

Wimsatt, James I. *Allegory and Mirror: Tradition and Structure in Middle English Literature*. New York: Pegasus, 1970. Pegasus Backgrounds in English Literature, gen. ed. J.R. Mulder.

Wittig, Kurt. *The Scottish Tradition in Literature*. Edinburgh and London: Oliver and Boyd, 1958.

Wood, H. Harvey, ed. *The Poems and Fables of Robert Henryson, Schoolmaster of Dunfermline*. 2nd ed. rev. Edinburgh: Oliver and Boyd, 1958; first published 1933.

Yearwood, Stephanie. "The Rhetoric of Narrative Rendering in Chaucer's *Troilus.*" *ChauR* 12.1 (1977): 27–37.

SCOTTISH STUDIES

Publications of the Scottish Studies Centre
of the Johannes Gutenberg-Universität Mainz
in Germersheim

General Editor: Horst W. Drescher

Bd./Vol. 1 Horst W. Drescher (ed.): Thomas Carlyle 1981. Papers Given at the International Thomas Carlyle Centenary Symposium. 1983.

Bd./Vol. 2 Manfred Malzahn: Aspects of Identity. The Contemporary Scottish Novel (1978-1981) as National Self-Expression. 1984.

Bd./Vol. 3 Horst W. Drescher/Joachim Schwend (eds.): Studies in Scottish Fiction. Nineteenth Century. 1985.

Bd./Vol. 4 Dietrich Strauss/Horst W. Drescher (eds.): Scottish Language and Literature, Medieval and Renaissance. Fourth International Conference 1984 – Proceedings. 1986.

Bd./Vol. 5 Horst W. Drescher (ed.): Literature and Literati. The Literary Correspondence and Notebooks of Henry Mackenzie. Volume 1 / Letters 1766-1827. 1989.

Bd./Vol. 6 Paola Bono: Radicals and Reformers in Late Eighteenth-Century Scotland. An Annotated Checklist of Books, Pamphlets, and Documents Printed in Scotland 1775-1800. 1989.

Bd./Vol. 7 Silke Böger: Traditions in Conflict. John MacDougall Hay's *Gillespie*. 1989.

Bd./Vol. 8 Horst W. Drescher/Hermann Völkel (eds.): Nationalism in Literature – Literarischer Nationalismus. Literature, Language and National Identity. 1989.

Bd./Vol. 9 Silvia Mergenthal: James Hogg: Selbstbild und Bild. Zur Rezeption des "Ettrick Shepherd". 1990.

Bd./Vol. 10 Joachim Schwend/Horst W. Drescher (eds.): Studies in Scottish Fiction. Twentieth Century. 1990.

Bd./Vol. 11 David Groves (ed.): James Hogg: Poetic Mirrors. Comprising the *Poetic Mirror* (1816) and *New Poetic Mirror* (1829-1831). 1990.

Bd./Vol. 12 Beat Witschi: Glasgow Urban Writing and Postmodernism. A Study of Alasdair Gray's Fiction. 1991.

Bd./Vol. 13 Susanne Hagemann: Die Schottische Renaissance. Literatur und Nation im 20. Jahrhundert. 1992.

Bd./Vol. 14 Joachim Schwend/Susanne Hagemann/Hermann Völkel (Hrsg.): Literatur im Kontext – Literature in Context. Festschrift für Horst W. Drescher. 1992.

Bd./Vol. 15 Rosemary Greentree: Reader, Teller and Teacher. The Narrator of Robert Henryson's Moral Fables. 1993.